U0503234

红山文化玉器鉴赏
A STUDY OF HONGSHAN CULTURE JADES

文物出版社
CULTURAL RELICS PRESS

A STUDY OF HONGSHAN CULTURE JADES

GUO DASHUN AND HONG DIANXU

CULTURAL RELICS PRESS

红山文化玉器鉴赏（增订本）

郭大顺 洪殿旭 编著

文物出版社

作者简介
Authors' Introduction

　　郭大顺（左），河北省张家口市人，1938年生。北京大学历史系考古专业研究生毕业。在辽宁省从事北方地区先秦考古研究，因发现牛河梁红山文化遗址而研究史前玉器。曾任辽宁省文化厅副厅长，现为中国考古学会名誉理事、国家文物鉴定委员会委员、辽宁省文史馆馆员、辽宁省文物考古研究所名誉所长。著有《红山文化》、《牛河梁遗址》、《玉器的起源与渔猎文化》、《从史前玉器研究成果看中国史前史》等论著。

Guo Dashun, born in Hebei Province in 1938, is Managing Director of Chinese Society of Archaeology, member with State Committee of Cultural Relics Authentication, and Honorary Director of Liaoning Provincial Institute of Cultural Relics and Archaeology. After graduating from Department of History, Peking University with MA degree in archaeology, he was engaged in pre-Qin archaeology in northern China's Liaoning Province for a long time. Since the discovery of Hongshan Culture site at Niuheliang, Guo became interested in prehistoric jades. He is the author of Hongshan Culture, Niuheliang Site, The Origin of Jades and the Culture of Fishing and Hunting, and Chinese Prehistoric History Reflected in Research Findings of Prehistoric Jades.

　　洪殿旭，辽宁省沈阳市人。曾任辽宁国际贸易公司副总经理、辽宁国际经济开发公司总经理和辽宁省戏剧家企业家事业家联谊会副会长，现任加拿大美大国际（集团）公司董事长、加拿大中国文物保护基金会会长、中国红山文化学会会长、中国收藏家协会专家委员会委员和理事、中国文物学会专家委员会委员和理事、中国文物保护基金会理事。在中国和加拿大收藏古代艺术品二十余年，现主要从事海外回流文物方面的事宜和工作。

　　在入住科学家花园后与辽宁省文物考古研究所名誉所长、研究员孙守道先生成为邻居，并在他的影响下开始学习、研究和收藏红山文化玉器。近年来，又得到了辽宁省文物考古研究所名誉所长、著名考古学家郭大顺先生的指导与帮助，逐步走上了收藏和研究并重的道路。于2010年与郭大顺主编《红山文化玉器鉴赏》一书。

Hong Dianxu, born in Shenyang, Liaoning Province, is President of Canada Media International Group, President of China Cultural Relics Protection Foundation in Canada, President of Hongshan Culture Association, Director and member of Experts Committee of China Association of Collectors, Honorary Director of China Cultural Relics Protection Foundation, and Honorary Director of Chinese Society of Cultural Relics. He was Deputy Manager of Liaoning International Trade Inc, General Manager of Liaoning International Economic Development Inc and vice Chairperson of Liaoning Provincial Association of Entrepreneurs, Industrialists, and Playwrights. Working in the past two decades in China and Canada in antiquities collection and trade, he is now engaged in importing overseas Chinese antiquities.

After moving into the Scientists Garden, Hong became the neighbour of Sun Shoudao, former Director of Liaoning Provincial Institute of Cultural Relics and Archaeology, and began to study and collect Hongshan Culture jades under Sun's influence. In recent years, with the help of Guo Dashun, archaeologist and Honorary Director of Liaoning Provincial Institute of Cultural Relics and Archaeology, he has become a collector and researcher of jades. He co-edited and published A Study of Hongshan Culture Jades with Guo Dashun in 2010.

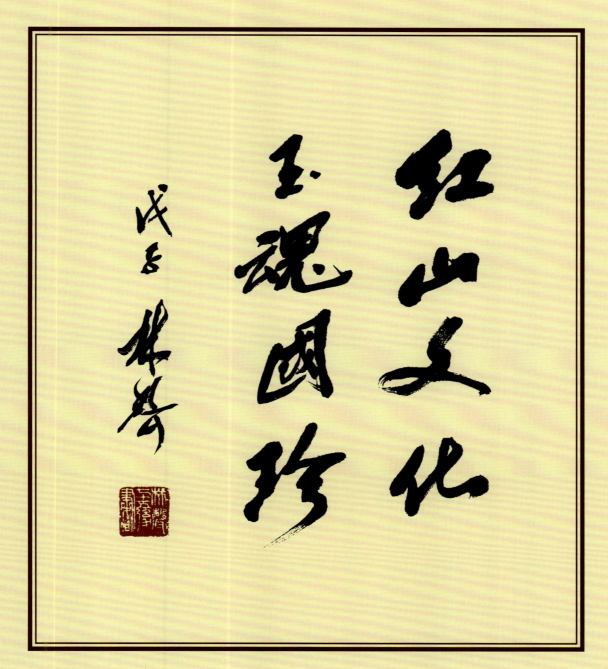

红山文化 玉魂国珍

林声
辽宁省政府原副省长
辽宁省政协原常务副主席

Lin Sheng

former Vice Governor of Liaoning Province

former Executive Deputy Chairman of Liaoning Political Consultative Conference

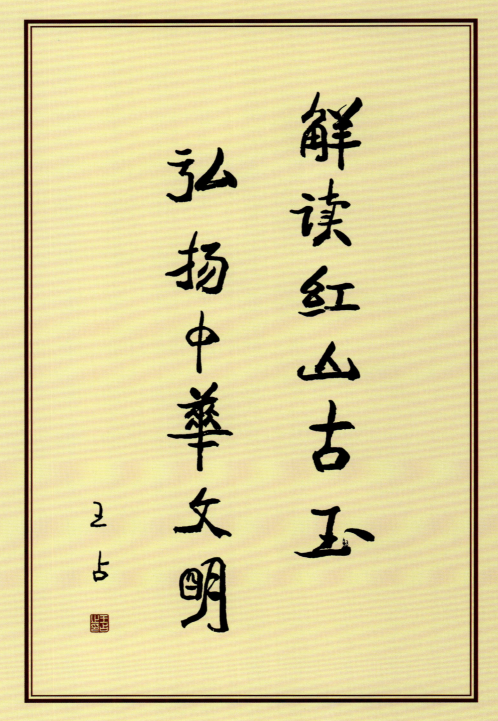

解读红山古玉
弘扬中华文明

王占

王占
内蒙古自治区原常务副主席
内蒙古自治区政协主席

Wang Zhan
former Executive Deputy Chairman of Inner Mongolia Autonomous Region
Chairman of Inner Mongolia Autonomous Region

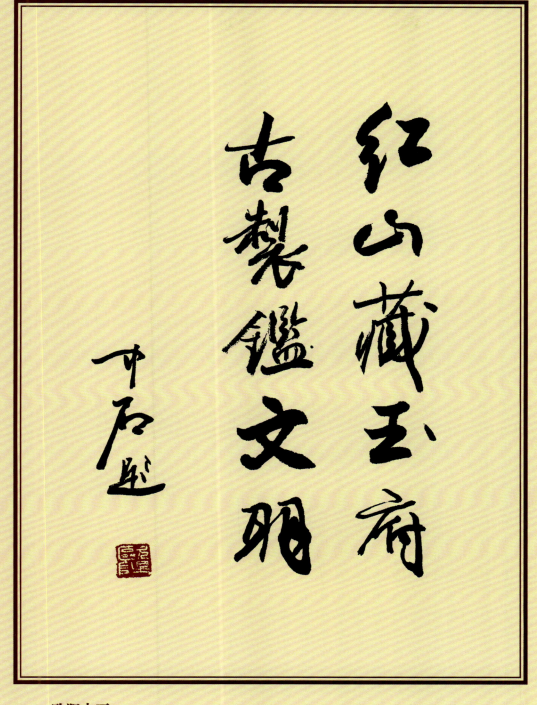

红山藏玉府
古製鑑文明

欧阳中石
中国书法研究院名誉院长
首都师范大学博士生导师

Ouyang Zhongshi

Honorary Director of Institute of Chinese Calligraphy and Ph.D. supervisor of
Capital Normal University

红山文化因内蒙古赤峰红山后遗址的发掘而得名，是主要分布于内蒙古东南部、辽宁西部及河北北部地区的新石器时代考古学文化，年代距今约6500~5000年。现正式考古发掘的红山文化玉器主要为红山文化晚期，距今约为5500~5000年。出土玉器的地点主要有辽宁朝阳的建平、凌源两县交界处的牛河梁遗址群，阜新县胡头沟、福兴地，喀左县东山嘴，赤峰敖汉旗草帽山、大五家小东山，内蒙古巴林右旗那斯台、羊场、巴彦查干苏木，巴林左旗葛家营子、尖山子，克什克腾旗南台子，翁牛特旗赛沁塔拉，林西县南沙窝子，以及宁城县打虎石水库。另有河北围场县下伙房、阳原县姜家梁等。

红山文化玉器主要器形有人物、动物、斜口筒形器、勾云形器、环、璧等类。从中反映出红山人已能用纯熟的片切割、圆雕、透雕等技法制造出内涵丰富、独具特色的玉器。"唯玉为葬"、"以玉事神"在红山文化中也有突出表现。

《红山文化玉器鉴赏》收录历年发现于以上地区、散见于全国乃至世界各地现存的红山文化玉器213件，并按以下类别对其进行了编排：考古发掘品、有出土单位的收集品、遗址收集品、有出土地点的收集品、有出土地区的收集品、其他珍贵收集品和资料部分，体现了科学严谨的态度。

牛河梁红山文化的祭坛和积石冢遗迹

Hongshan Culture Altar and
Stone Mounds at the Niuheliang Site

The Hongshan Culture is a type of Neolithic archaeological culture dating to about 6,500–5,000 years ago. Its remains are mainly found in southeastern Inner Mongolia Autonomous Region, western Liaoning Province, and northern Hebei Province. Most of the Hongshan jades discovered in archaeological excavations date to the late Hongshan Culture of about 5,500–5,000 years ago. These jades come from Liaoning (including the Niuheliang sites complex on the border of Jianping County and Lingyuan County in Chaoyang City, Hutougou and Fuxingdi in Fuxin County, and Dongshanzui in Kazuo County) and Inner Mongolia (including Caomaoshan, Dawujia and Xiaodongshan in Aohan Banner in Chifeng City, Nasitai, Yangchang and Bayanchagansumu in Bairin Right Banner, Gejiayingzi and Jianshanzi in Bairin Left Banner, Nantaizi in Keshiketeng Banner, Sanxingtala in Wengniute Banner, Nanshawozi in Linxi County and Dahushi reservoir in Ningcheng County), as well as Hebei (Xiahuofang in Weichang County and Jiangjialiang in Yangyuan County).The Hongshan jades are made in the shapes of human figure, animal, hoof, hook and cloud, ring, and bi disc, etc., demonstrating the skillful cutting, carving, and openwork techniques mastered by the Hongshan people. The Hongshan jades were often used as burial objects or in worshiping. *A Study of Hongshan Culture Jades* introduces 213 pieces of Hongshan jades discovered in the above-mentioned locations and now collected by Chinese or overseas institutions. The objects in discussion are arranged carefully in seven categories: archaeological findings, collections unearthed from archaeological points, collections from archaeological sites, collections unearthed from certain sites, collections unearthed from certain regions, other important collections, and supplements.

编辑委员会
EDITORIAL BOARD

主 任	**Editors-in-chief**
白立忱	Bai Lichen
林 声 王 占	Lin Sheng, Wang Zhan

编委成员（按姓氏笔画排序）　**Editors**(in order of Chinese characters)

于宝东	于建设	王梅生	Yu Baodong, Yu Jianshe, Wang Meisheng,
王嗣洲	韦尔申	乌 兰	Wang Sizhou, Wei Ershen, Wu Lan,
白丽民	田茂峰	朱乃诚	Bai Limin, Tian Maofeng, Zhu Naicheng,
吕学明	齐 玮	许勇翔	Lv Xueming, Qi Wei, Xu Yongxiang,
许 超	刘 宁	刘国祥	Xu Chao, Liu Ning, Liu Guoxiang,
闫 娟	孙 亭	成胜泉	Yan Juan, Sun Ting, Cheng Shengquan,
李水城	李龙彬	李 兵	Li Shuicheng, Li Longbin, Li Bing,
李 凯	李 莉	宋志刚	Li Kai, Li Li, Song Zhigang,
宋 建	赵萧萧	张广文	Song Jian, Zhao Xiaoxiao, Zhang Guangwen,
张 尉	苏布德	杜 江	Zhang Wei, Su Bude, Du Jiang,
沈军山	杨凯夫	武俊玲	Shen Junshan, Yang Kaifu, Wu Junling,
孟昭凯	周高亮	周晓晶	Meng Zhaokai, Zhou Gaoliang, Zhou Xiaojing,
郑振香	青格勒	姚玉柱	Zheng Zhenxiang, Qing Gele, Yao Yuzhu,
侯文玉	娄 玮	姜 涛	Hou Wenyu, Lou Wei, Jiang Tao,
钱 玲	徐 琳	徐春苓	Qian Ling, Xu Lin, Xu Chunling,
高 炜	郭富纯	盛为人	Gao Wei, Guo Fuchun, Sheng Weiren,
常素霞	黄翠梅	程秀岩	Chang Suxia, Huang Cuimei, Cheng Xiuyan

增订本出版说明

一　本书增订本共增加标本22件。包括原书收入的191件（其中正文部分148件，资料部分43件），增订本共收入红山文化玉器213件（其中正文部分172件，资料部分41件）。

二　增订本增加的22件标本中，有正式发掘品1件，其他珍贵收集品13件，因图片收集方面的原因收于资料部分的8件。另由于图片收集方面的改善，从原书资料部分转入正文部分10件，其中转入正文正式发掘品3件，转入正文遗址收集品1件，转入正文有出土地点收集品1件，转入正文其他珍贵收集品5件。

　　这样增订本收入的考古发掘品，包括原书的47件标本，共收入考古发掘品48件。考古发掘品以外所收其他标本，包括原书的144件标本，增订本共收入165件。

　　考古发掘品中，有胡头沟和牛河梁遗址前期发掘品以及各地晚于红山文化遗存的考古发掘品，还有查海遗址发掘的部分先红山文化玉器。其他标本分两大部分，一是各地博物馆收藏的有遗址和遗址单位及遗址所在村镇、县市记录的收集品，这部分共68件（其中资料部分5件），一是海内外博物馆的其他珍贵收集品，这部分共97件（其中资料部分32件），海内外博物馆的其他珍贵收集品绝大部分为早年收藏并于20世纪80年代前发表过的收藏品。

三　分类。由于本书所收大多数标本的收藏过程与考古发掘和调查有关，所以在对标本进行分类时，没有完全按照一般图录所采用的依器物形态分类，而是采取考古关系优先的标准，即分别按考古发掘品与有出土单位的收集品、遗址收集品、有出土地点的收集品、有出土地区的收集品和其他珍贵收集品进行分类，资料部分也依上述类别划分。这样分类，也与红山文化玉器的发现史相符合。

四　考古发掘品排序。凡红山文化遗址的考古发掘品，均按出土的年代排序。其他不同时代的遗址的考古发掘品，则按遗存的年代排序。

五　地区和收藏单位排序。辽宁西部和内蒙古东南部是红山文化玉器分布的中心区，也是本书所收标本较多的地区，所以在地区和收藏单位中排序在前。

六　器物名称统一使用现名称。部分器物将原发表时的名称予以保留。部分海外藏品原发表的英文名称也予以保留。

七　收藏单位为本书提供的标本文字说明大都予以引用。部分标本还引用了原发表时的文字说明。

八　标本编号。除考古发掘品使用发掘编号以外，对各博物馆和文物单位的收集品，也尽量将单位藏品的原编号予以保留。

九　英文翻译。文字说明部分除了器物描述以外的，都作了英译。海外提供的英文文字说明也予以保留。

ILLUSTRATION OF ENLARGED EDITION OF *A STUDY OF HONGSHAN CULTURE JADES*

I. 22 pieces of Hongshan jades have been added to the enlarged edition, plus 191 pieces in the original edition (148 pieces in main contents and 43 pieces in supplements). Therefore, 213 pieces of Hongshan jades are listed in the enlarged edition, including 172 pieces in main contents and 41 pieces in supplements.

II. Among the 22 additional pieces of Hongshan jades, 1 piece is put into archaeological findings and 13 pieces are put into other important collections. Besides, 8 pieces are put into supplements in lack of proper illustrations. What's more, 10 pieces have been transferred from supplements to the main contents, including 3 pieces in archaeological findings, 1 piece in collections from archaeological sites, 1 piece in collections unearthed from certain sites, 5 pieces in other important collections. In conclusion, the enlarged edition covers altogether 48 pieces of Hongshan jades in archaeological findings, including 47 pieces in the original edition. Other than archaeological findings, 165 pieces of Hongshan jades are listed in the enlarged edition, including 144 pieces in the original edition. Archaeological findings cover early findings from Hutougou and Niuheliang sites, findings from other sites later than Hongshan Culture and some pre-Hongshan Culture findings from Chahai site. Besides, other specimens are mainly divided into two parts. Museum collections with records of names of sites and their specific locations in villages, towns, counties and cities accounting to 68 pieces (5 pieces in supplements) and other important overseas museum collections accounting to 97 pieces (32 pieces in supplements). Most of the latter were collected by overseas museums a long time ago and came into publication in the 1980s.

III. Category. Since the collection of most jade objects contained in the book is related to archaeological findings and investigations, archaeological relation takes priority in terms of putting the jade objects into category, instead of the shape standard usually adopted by catalogues. Therefore, the book is categorized into six sections, archaeological findings, collections unearthed from archaeological points, collections from archaeological sites, collections unearthed from certain sites, collections unearthed from certain regions and other important collections. Supplements are also categorized as above-mentioned. Archaeological sites, collection regions and collection institutions are factors considered in secondary category. Such category suits the history of finding Hongshan Culture jades.

IV. Order of archaeological findings. Archaeological findings of Hongshan Culture jades are listed based on their dates of excavation. Archaeological findings from other sites of different times are arranged according to their times of sites.

V. Order of regions and collection institutions. Western Liaoning Province and southeastern Inner Mongolia make up central distribution area of Hongshan Culture jades, which also provides a great amount of jade articles in the book and thus rank first.

VI. Names of the jade objects adopt their current names. Names of certain objects in original publications are preserved, as well as English names of certain overseas collections when first publicized.

VII. Explanatory notes for the jade objects provided by collection institutions are mostly cited. Certain objects also cite the original publicized notes.

VIII. Numbering jade objects. Archaeological findings continue to use their archaeological numbers. For collections from museums and units of cultural relics, their original numbers are also preserved.

IX. English translation. Except the descriptions of the objects, all explanatory notes have been translated into English. Overseas English explanatory notes are also saved.

目 录

前 言　郭大顺 ……………………………………………… 016

◎ 1　考古发掘品 …………………………………………… 034

◎ 2　有出土单位的收集品 ………………………………… 080

◎ 3　遗址收集品 …………………………………………… 092

◎ 4　有出土地点的收集品 ………………………………… 118

◎ 5　有出土地区的收集品 ………………………………… 140

◎ 6　其他珍贵收集品 ……………………………………… 156

◎ 7　资料部分 ……………………………………………… 220

附录：玉器鉴定的基本方法　洪殿旭 …………………… 236

后 记　洪殿旭 …………………………………………… 245

CONTENTS

Preface   Guo Dashun ···································· 022

◎ 1   Archaeological Findings ···································· 034

◎ 2   Collections Unearthed from Archaeological Points ···························· 080

◎ 3   Collections from Archaeological Sites ···························· 092

◎ 4   Collections Unearthed from Certain Sites ···························· 118

◎ 5   Collections Unearthed from Certain Regions ···························· 140

◎ 6   Other Important Collections ···························· 156

◎ 7   Supplements ···································· 220

Appendix: Basic Methods of Jades Identifying   Hong Dianxu ········· 240

Acknowledgements   Hong Dianxu ···································· 247

前 言

◎ 郭大顺

经林声先生（辽宁省原副省长）介绍，我结识了洪殿旭先生。初次见面，谈起他有感于辽宁出有红山文化玉器，特别是他的夫人迟小秋女士（京剧名家）家乡阜新市的查海遗址，出有迄今最早的真玉器。由此，洪先生很希望与我合作出版一本关于红山文化玉器鉴赏的书籍。

想到目前红山文化玉器除辽西朝阳市牛河梁遗址正式出土的以外，散见于各地的也不少，还没有一本集中介绍的书籍。如能收集出版，不仅对于鉴赏，就是对于红山文化玉器的研究，无疑都是一件好事。为此，我向他建议，如编写一本鉴赏红山文化玉器的书，那就把各地博物馆流传有序的藏品收集在一起，包括已知海外收藏的红山文化玉器，以此作为这本书的主要内容。这一设想可能与他原来的想法有些不同，主要是增加了材料收集的难度，不过，他很尊重我的意见，就按这个思路开始了准备工作。由于散见的红山文化玉器收藏于多个单位，多是文博系统的，但也有教育系统的，还有海外收藏的，洪先生则往来于各地，广泛联系结识文博考古界各方面人士，努力收集起来。还为经费的筹措而奔忙。那种执著精神，令我佩服，也加深了我们合作的基础。

近几年，为拓宽玉器研究领域，各方面都在对古代玉器研究现状进行回顾。起步晚，进展快，是对中国古代玉器研究史的准确概括。如大家经常所议论的那样，虽然玉器的收藏研究也起步较早，但长期以来，对玉器的重视程度远不如其他类别，如青铜器、瓷器等，在博物馆藏品中，玉器被列入杂项，在考古发掘报告中，被作为"小件"，列于文章最后加以简略介绍，还有将玉器甚至具代表性或十分精美的玉器，放在石器中介绍。这种情况一直持续到20世纪70年代，也就是说，古代玉器研究得到重视，不过是近30年来的事，但研究的成果却已令人刮目相看。不仅发表的资料越来越丰富，出版的有关书籍越来越多，而且研究进程步步深入，已从传世玉器到出土玉器，进而提出玉文化和玉学的新思路，甚至在以考古资料复原历史的任务中，玉器所起的作用也越来越明显，由此玉器在考古学和文物博物馆事业中的地位自然很快得到提高。在这一急速转变过程中，史前玉器的考古新发现起到领头羊的作用，而红山文化玉器又在其中扮演着主力军的角色。

我对玉器原没有专门研究，也就是因为发掘和研究红山文化，经常接触到玉器，才不断有所体会，并加入到玉器研究的大军中来。不过，主要还是作为考古学的一个组成部分来进行研究的。如果说与玉器鉴赏有点关系的研究成果，可围绕红山文化玉器在选料、制作、埋葬中所体现的对玉本质的表达，谈几点看法。

选料。台南艺术大学黄翠梅、叶贵玉两位先生在2004年内蒙古赤峰"红山文化国际学术研讨会"上曾发表一篇文章，以为红山文化玉器与良渚文化玉器在尺寸大小、造型风格上的差异，与选料有关，前者以河磨玉为主，后者以开采山料为主，是很有启示的观点。我们在编写牛河梁遗址发掘报告时，有机会全面观察牛河梁遗址出土玉器，发现其中玉料较好的，大都采自河磨玉。河磨玉是大自然的杰作，不仅是石之精华，也是玉之精华，是最能表现玉本质的部分。虽然因玉料来之不易，红山文化用河磨玉做成的玉器，体积一般不大，造型也受到制约，而且遗有大量皮壳部分。但红山人善于将劣势转变为优势，如对待玉石的皮壳，凡红山文化玉器中选用河磨玉料的玉器，其主要部分为本色，皮壳总是尽量被安排在器的边缘或末端，形成绿色为主、红色陪衬的布局，有的甚至可能已是俏色的做法。红山文化对色彩的重视可以其他实例作为旁证：在牛河梁祭祀遗址群的积石冢中，规模较大的冢群有用白色石灰岩石垒砌的积石冢和近旁以红色玄武岩立置的红色祭坛相组合，白色石灰岩石砌起的积石冢上成行排列着红色筒形陶器群，陶器红地上绘黑彩或红地上涂朱、涂黑等等，这些色彩不同的元素常以对比的形式出现，说明红山人对自然界各种色彩辨别的敏感性和相互谐调的合理掌握，看来，对色彩的巧妙利用已经成为红山人信仰的一个重要组成部分。所以在玉器选料和设计制作时巧用天然玉的色彩，既突显玉的本色，又加强了玉器的装饰与点缀，是顺理成章的事。当然，这也增加了红山文化玉器的艺术内涵和感染力。

磨光。这本是玉器制作的必备程序，但红山文化玉器在这方面似乎特别用功。观察发现，红山文化时期玉料的加工已普遍使用片切割成材技术，经切割后的玉材，棱角锐利，形状趋于规正，但是红山人并不直接利用这一成形的有利条件，而总是要再加以磨光使这些棱边圆而光滑。同样，红山人已掌握了管钻法钻孔技术，钻孔后孔缘的锐棱也都要再加磨光，使孔缘既不失规正，又突出了圆润的效果。再就是用料较大、体积也较大的斜口筒形玉器，以线切割掏大而甚长的孔，掏孔后的壁面面积大而甚薄，不过仍要对内、外壁都细加磨制，这种特意精磨加工的情况尤其见于玉璧。红山文化玉器中玉璧也较为常见，其特点不仅内外缘和壁面都经磨制，而且将玉璧做成外方圆内圆的形状，玉璧是从史前到战国秦汉玉器中持续时间最长的一类玉器，但全都是内外孔缘直壁、壁面平整的定制，唯红山文化玉璧为内圆外方、壁面鼓而内外边缘薄似刃。对这些费时又费工的现象的合理解释是，设计制作者是要有意以磨光来突出玉的质地，从而表达某种特定的观念。

与磨光的大量使用相应的，是对饰纹的慎重。红山人对器物外表进行装饰的意识本来很强，在夹砂粗陶罐上满饰整齐密布的各式各样的压印纹就充分表明这一点。在玉器上饰纹虽然比在陶器上饰纹难度大得多，不过从已发现有纹饰的玉器来看，红山人已掌握了在玉器上刻划复杂花纹的技术。但他们对在玉器上刻划装饰却极为慎重，一般除对动物的头部和鸟类的羽翅等进行必要的刻划以外，所见装饰主要是采用减地阳纹式的技法。这又可以分几种情况，一是用减地法表现动物头部五官，如玉龟和玉鸟，各部位皆不甚显露，仅触之有感，却很准确。二是在平面上显示立体感。如牛河梁出土的一件大型玉凤，是在平板上以直线为主成纹，由于采用减地手法，既甚为简洁，又克服了平面直线的呆滞，最大限度地体现出羽翅和尾羽的层次。三是在勾云形玉器或有弯度的玉件如玉臂饰等薄板状玉器的表面上，以减地法做出有似瓦沟状的凹槽，可称瓦沟纹，这种瓦沟纹的宽与窄、深与浅多十分均匀，起到随光线的变化若隐若现的奇特效果，其中目前所发现的红山文化玉器中尺寸最长的一件勾云形玉器，长而甚薄，要从两面通体磨沟，沟纹槽必然很浅，然而所起的脊棱线条，清晰而流畅，都十分到位。不过由于纹槽甚浅，一般情况下只能看到花纹的局部，要想看到全貌，只有将光线调到十分准确的角度。此外，刻划有纹的玉件，也常与这种沟槽相间相隔，起到相互衬托作用，如玉雕龙的首部。

以上装饰工艺的制作难度都要远高于其他刻划纹饰，却可以对人的视觉产生极大冲击，那就是随着光线照射角度的变化，使这些纹饰时隐时现，从而最大限度地突出了以玉质本身来表现一些特殊效果，如立体感、层次感特别是神秘感。可见，红山文化玉器制作上的这些特殊处理方法和由此而形成的独特风格，并非技术上的原始性，确是一种刻意追求，目的是不靠过多的外加的人为因素，就使玉器自身的特性，得以充分表现出来。

突出玉的特性还体现在红山文化的埋葬习俗上，那就是"唯玉为葬"。"唯玉为葬"，即墓中只葬玉器而不葬一般史前文化所常见的陶器、石器等。牛河梁遗址已发掘4个地点，发掘近百座墓，有随葬品的墓占到一半左右。这批有随葬品的墓葬中，同时有玉器和陶器随葬的和同时有玉与石器随葬的各只1座墓，只随葬陶器不随葬玉器的也只3座墓，其余的墓葬都只葬玉器，只随葬玉器的墓占到有随葬品墓葬的近90%。牛河梁遗址积石冢中以玉器随葬为主的这种情况，还有依时代和等级而有所变化的规律，即只随葬玉器的墓集中于晚期墓和规模越大的墓全部都只葬玉器。说明只葬玉器，是牛河梁遗址埋葬习俗的一个具有代表性的特点。

这里要强调的是，史前诸文化的墓葬，都是以陶器为主要随葬品的，也不乏用石器随葬，只有红山文化是个例外。本来红山文化已具备了相当发达的制石和制陶工艺，大型打制石器、磨制石器、细石器三大类石器并重和石犁耜的大量使用，为同时期其他史前文化所不及。细石器更讲究选料的硬度、色泽、纹理和通体精细加工，有的已是精致的工艺品。红山文化的制陶业，有以具东北文化特征的压印"之"字纹陶和受中原仰韶文化影响的彩陶器这北、南两种文化融为一体的陶器群，巨大的积石冢上有立置陶筒形器的做法，这些陶筒形器，个体较大，成行排列，动辄数百近千，它们已属批量生产的产品。尤其是牛河梁遗址出现了一批与祭祀有关的特异形陶器，如积石冢和女神庙出土的造型复杂的"祖"形器、女神庙及附近窖穴出土的熏炉器盖和彩陶方器，都是烧制技术甚高的祭礼器。但在红山文化墓葬中，却极少有这些高等级的陶、石器随葬，而只葬玉器。把这种独具特色的葬制放在当时社会大背景下考察，红山文化正处于由原始社会向文明社会过渡的社会变革时期，墓葬规模及随葬品的数量、质量是反映人与人等级差别最主要的标准，该文化不葬或少葬与生产、生活有关的石器和陶器，只葬非实用的玉器，说明当时在表达人与人之间等级地位时，对精神领域不同层次的特殊重视，要远高于对物质财富的占有，也表明红山文化对玉器的认识已经达到一个高峰。

总之，红山文化玉从选河磨玉为料、制作重磨光而轻饰纹，特别是"唯玉为葬"的埋葬习俗，都是围绕着一个目的，那就是使玉的圆润、纯洁、光泽等本质得以最大限度的发挥，史前时期的玉器是用以通神的，所谓"以玉事神"，古人在自然界众多石料中独选择玉作为通神工具，是意识到玉在石料中属于中性物质，玉所具有的温而润等自然特性，是最符合与神联系的，因为沟通需要和谐，可以达到与天地神人沟通的最佳效果，这种靠自然物的特性来达到人与神之间沟通的纯真而神圣的思想观念，是古人尊重大自然的体现。研究还发现，实现人与神沟通的使者是巫，巫者既然是玉器的主要使用者，也必然参与玉器的设计制作，在这一过程中，巫作为群体中智慧与德行的集大成者，也同时赋予了玉器以道德价值的观念，这同此后孔子时代以玉的各种特性表达人的德性的"以玉比德"的种种记载，自有其承续的脉络可寻。

以上只是鉴赏红山文化玉器的一个方面。如果说对红山人所创造的玉文化的本质已有所触及，那就是通过这样逐层思考，既可了解红山文化玉器的社会价值，欣赏其艺术价值，又可揭示当时人与人的关系，人与自然的关系。以古比今，在当今和未来社会的飞速发展中，人与自然相处，人与人相处以及人自身修身养性的调整，在人们的生活和社会活动中越来越提到重要位置，我们在鉴赏红山文化玉器的时候，在被其艺术魅力感染的同时，不是可以对当今社会提出的这些迫切需要回答的问题有更多的领悟吗？进一步而言，在鉴赏时追求心态的纯真、营造和谐的气氛非常重要，因为只有在那种美妙的境界中，方可体会被古人视为"神物"的玉器的精髓所在。

以上是我在研究玉器主要是红山文化玉器的点滴体会，愿与红山文化玉器研究者爱好者共勉。

PREFACE

◎ Guo Dashun

Mr. Lin Sheng, the esteemed curator of the Cultural History Museum and the former vice-governor of Liaoning Province in charge of cultural affairs, introduced me to Mr. Hong Dianxu, an entrepreneur from Liaoning. When I first met him, Mr.Hong talked about the Hongshan jades discovered in Liaoning, especially the earlier jades unearthed from the Chahai site in Fuxin city, which is the hometown of his wife, Ms. Chi Xiaoqiu, a descendant of the Cheng branch of the Peking Opera. Mr. Hong expressed his desire to publish a book on the appreciation of Hongshan jades in collaboration with myself.

I have long thought of the fact that many of the acknowledged Hongshan jades, with the exception of those unearthed from the Niuheliang site in Chaoyang city of west Liaoning, are dispersed in different places and that there is no one book published that has included them all. I thought it would be a great step forward if such a book could be published, which would enable both further appreciation of, and more research into, Hongshan jades. I therefore suggested that such a book be compiled, which would systematically gather together all such Hongshan jades from different museums, including those overseas. Although my suggestion differed from Mr. Hong's initial idea, and had the additional difficulty of collecting data from overseas, he accepted my proposal and we began the work according to my suggestion. Hongshan jades are now held in many different places, most of them in museums, but some of them at universities, and some overseas. Mr. Hong was very diligent in getting in touch with a lot of different people from different organizations in order to further the collection of the data and for fund raising. His perseverance impressed me deeply and strengthened my desire to cooperate with him.

In recent years, in order to further the horizons of research, some reviews on ancient jades studies have been published. "A late start but fast progress" is a phrase that can be seen as an appropriate summary of the history of jade studies. As has been discussed, though, the collecting and appreciation of ancient jades has an early start generally but not enough attention has been paid to jade studies, compared with bronzes and porcelain collections. For a long time within museums the jades were often labelled as "miscellaneous objects". In archaeological excavation monographs, the jades were generally listed after the last chapter, so that only a brief description was given of them, and even some elegant jades were categorized within the lists of stone tools. This situation was not changed until the 1970s. That is to say, the emphasis on jade studies has only had a short history dating to the last thirty years or so. However, a great deal of remarkable progress has been made since then. More and more jade materials have been collected and books published. The research process has been extended from collected jades to excavated jades, and a new perspective for jade cultural studies and the science of jade has been proposed. Jade studies have achieved a much more prominent position in terms of archaeological research. This is one reason why jades are now more important in archaeological and museum studies. In the process of this rapid transformation, the newly discovered prehistoric jades from archaeological excavations have played a leading role, particularly the Hongshan jades.

I am not a jade research specialist but I have excavated and studied Hongshan culture so I have been able to touch these jades, accumulated experience, and engaged with relevant research groups. However, apart from archaeological studies, which relates to an appreciation of jades in this context, I feel that studies of Hongshan jades should be focused on their choice of raw materials, their process of manufacturing, and the burial context as follows：

CHOICE OF RAW MATERIALS．Huang Cuimei and Ye Guiyu pointed out at a international conference on Hongshan Culture in Chifeng, Inner Mongolia in 2004 that the differences between the Hongshan and Liangzhu jades, in their sizes and shapes, can be seen as a result of the difference in the choice of raw materials. The Hongshan people preferred to use river jade (pebbles) but Liangzhu jades are mainly composed of mountain jade resources. This is an interesting suggestion. When I was editing the archaeological excavation monograph about the Niuheliang site, I had an opportunity to observe all the unearthed jades from it and found that those jades of good-quality were mainly from river boulders. The river jades can be viewed as natural masterpieces. Due to a lack of resources, Hongshan jades made from river pebbles are relatively smaller in size and restrained in their shapes. Even some of the original jade skin was left on some parts of the jades. However, the Hongshan people were very clever in making use of this skin as an enhancement for the design of the jade. The core of the jade boulder was worked as the main part of the jade and the jade skin was always masterfully used on the exterior so as to achieve a colour scheme of green or red colours as the principal hue, and other colours were used for the embellishment of the object. The variety of colours used could even be seen as deliberate in some cases of the Hongshan jades. The Hongshan people's particular preoccupation with colour can be discerned from other evidence. For example, in the Niuheliang stone burial groups, the large-scale tombs were mainly made from white limestone with red basalt sacrificial altars nearby and red, thick, cylindrical pots stood above them in rows. The surfaces of these pots were always painted with black or red decorative patterns. This presentation of contrasting colours in groups, indicates that the Hongshan people were particularly sensitive to natural colours and could make very good use of them. This perhaps shows that colour played an important part in the Hongshan religious beliefs. Therefore it is no wonder that the colour of the natural jade was emphasized in the choice of the raw material, and in the design pattern for the purpose of both an appreciation of the nature of the jade material and the enhancement of the decoration. Such factors should be taken into account when we study and talk about the Hongshan jades as well.

POLISHING. Although this was a necessary step for all jade working, it seems that for the Hongshan Culture this was particularly important. After detailed observation, we can see that cutting marks on the raw materials were generally popular in Hongshan Culture and this would be beneficial for making regular jade objects with clear-cut edges. However, it seems that the Hongshan people were not keen on this. Instead they preferred to polish hard edges so as to make them feel smooth. Meanwhile, Hongshan jade workers were good at drilling with hollow drills. But they also liked to polish the edges of holes to achieve a regular but rounded effect. Another example of their specialties includes the relatively large-sized, tubular-shaped jade with an oblique end (horse's hoof shaped jade). The large and long hollow was made by thread saws. But after the cutting, the jade was polished thoroughly on both the inner and outer surfaces of the jade, despite its thinness. This particular emphasis on polishing technique can also be recognized in the working of the disc-shaped *bi* jade which was also a popular jade type in Hongshan Culture. The surface of this kind of jade was polished on both the inner and outer sides of the edges and the jade outer shape was slightly squared, rather than circular, but with a round inner hole. The disc in jade was prevalent for a long time, from prehistory to the historical Warring States Period, and through the Qin and Han Dynasties. But most of them were made with regular frame both for inner holes and outer edges. Only Hongshan disc-shaped jades are round on the inside and square on the outside with convex surfaces and their edges are as thin as a knife blade. The explanation for using such a time-consuming manufacturing technique suggests that the Hongshan jade workers wanted to polish the jade surfaces so as to make the best possible presentation of the jade's inherent qualities.

As well as the widely used polishing techniques, the linear decoration on the jades is an important element. Essentially the Hongshan people had strong ideas about decorating the surfaces of their artifacts. For example, the surfaces of pots with coarse sand inclusions were extensively covered by various different patterns. Although it was more difficult to carve on the surface of jade than pottery, the

Hongshan people mastered the techniques necessary to work complex decorative patterns on their jades. They carefully limited the carving and this was only used in indispensable places such as for the heads of animals, or the wings of birds, using an abrasive method of working. Three examples of such detailed work can be distinguished. The first is the use of this decorative technique to represent animal heads, such as those on the jade turtles and birds. Though the decoration is not easily discernible, often only revealed by touching, the characteristics of these features are quite accurately depicted. Secondly, another feature is the way the Hongshan people showed embossed effect on flat surfaces. As an example, a phoenix-shaped jade unearthed from the Niuheliang site was decorated with straight line patterns on the flat surface. On account of the abrasive working techniques applied, the decorative patterns are simple but impressive and well demarcate the different levels of the wings and tail feathers. The third is the hooked-cloud jade pendant shape or the thin jade arm-guard. The patterns on these kinds of jades are called "roof-tile" shaped decorations and they were made by the method of abrasive working. The different levels of depth between the convex lines are evenly distributed over the jade surfaces which therefore produced magical effects when light is reflected on different angles of the jade. The longest hooked-cloud jade ornament that has been unearthed from Hongshan Culture site is long and thin with hollow grooves on both sides. These grooves are shallow, but clear, and have smooth forming ridge lines which can only be seen in detail under the right angle of light. In addition, some jade ornaments with carved decorative lines are decorated with lines and grooves in between, such as the decorative pattern on the head of the jade dragon.

The difficulties of the decorative technique described above are much greater than other such techniques but it is very striking. Under different lighting scenarios, these decorations appear and disappear as if they are harbouring some secretive aspect of the jade material itself. Therefore, these particular jade working techniques and the styles that originated from them, are not primitive at all but rather a method of enhancing the nature of the jade material without any sense of artificiality.

The importance of jade to these people can be recognized from the burial customs of the Hongshan Culture, especially the artifacts buried in tombs. Most of the artifacts buried in Hongshan tombs are jades, which is quite different from the other prehistoric cultures where pottery and stone tools were more frequently found. At the present date four locations within the Niuheliang site have been excavated and nearly one hundred tombs have been discovered, within which complex there is only one tomb buried with both jade and stone, three tombs with pottery only, and the rest are all tombs containing jades, which therefore comprises nearly ninety percent of the tombs in total. What is more, this burial pattern obviously changed over time and according to the rank of the person buried. For example, the tombs containing only jades are much more frequent in the later periods and in the higher ranking burials. This indicates that burying jades in tombs was one of the typical burial customs of the Niuheliang people.

What should be emphasized here is that most of the prehistoric tombs contained pottery or stone tools and only the Hongshan Culture tombs were an exception. The Hongshan people had the ability to produce sophisticated pottery and stone tools. Chipped stone, polished stone, and microlithic assemblages are all popular in the Hongshan Culture, especially a type of large stone plow seldom found in other prehistoric cultures. The microlithic assemblages show a careful choice of material, emphasizing the hardness, colour and texture of the material and most of this lithic material had been carefully processed to produce elaborate objects. The Hongshan Culture has advanced pottery-making techniques using mixed decorative styles such as a Z-shaped pattern in the northeast, and colourful painted patterns in central China. The large, thin, cylindrical pots were usually aligned on the top of stone tombs in numbers of similar sizes, which may indicate mass-production at this time. In addition, some particular pottery for ritual ceremonies has been unearthed from the Niuheliang site, such as the complex-designed, penis-shaped pots from the stone tombs and the Goddess Temple, incense burner pots, and square painted pots from the Goddess Temple and the ash pit nearby. However, in the Hongshan burials, valuable stone tools and pottery are seldom discovered. If we consider this to be a unique burial custom within the social context of that time, we can conclude that the Hongshan Culture existed during the transitional period between that of the primitive egalitarian society and the later hierarchical, more complex society. The scale of the tombs, together with the quality and quantities of artifacts buried in these tombs, indicate the social hierarchies that existed at that time. The Hongshan people preferred to bury jades that had no practical use, instead of the pottery or stone tools which had a use in everyday life. This indicates some idea of what people were thinking at that time, and that the possession of wealth in Hongshan Culture was represented by the jades, and that these also represented social status. And also from such burials we can see that the Hongshan people had a profound knowledge of jade working at a very high level.

In conclusion, from the choice of the raw material, the polishing techniques, the decorative patterns, and especially the custom of exclusively burying jades, the result of complex techniques of the Hongshan jade working is to make the best use of the jade material, emphasizing its smoothness, purity, and luster so as to satisfy the ancient spirits to the greatest extent possible. In prehistoric times, jade was primarily used to communicate with and to worship the gods. The ancient people chose jade from other natural stone materials for their worshipping of the gods because jade has the essential quality of smoothness, which seemed to be regarded as an essential for communication with the gods. The communication between heaven, the gods, and human beings need a harmonious atmosphere. The innocent and sacred notions to use the nature of jades to realize these communications reflected the worship and obeisance of the ancient people to the nature. As we know, shamans were the agents used in communicating between the gods and human beings and they must have been involved in the jade working process where they acted as important people of intelligence and virtue, thereby endowing jade with this virtue also. This aspect of jade can be related to the later Confucian periods with its association of jade with the virtues of noblemen.

What has been mentioned above is only part of an appreciation of Hongshan jades. An appreciation of the essence of Hongshan jades is perhaps a step which will lead to a better understanding of the social value of Hongshan jades. By appreciating its artistic value we can proceed to try and understand the relationship between different human beings and the relationship between human beings and nature itself. Today with the rapid development of modern society, if we are to learn from the past, the harmony between human beings and nature, the relationship between human beings, and the development of one's personal virtue are more and more important in people's lives and social activities. If we appreciate Hongshan jades and are influenced by their artistic values, perhaps we can achieve a greater understanding of the many important questions raised by modern society, What is more, a spirit of purity and the building of harmonious atmospheres are crucial for the appreciation of jade. And only within such an environment can we really understand the true nature of the jade material, a material worshiped by the ancients as something sacred.

That is what I have been learning from my studies of Hongshan jades and I wish to share this with all Hongshan jade researchers and lovers of jade generally.

锡林浩特

黄岗梁▲2029

西拉   木   伦   河

科尔沁沙地

浑善达克沙地

七

老

图

赤峰

山

努

鲁

儿

虎

山

4

14

3

2

1

6

5

11

7

10

9

8

12

朝阳

大

凌

河

燕

承德

山

▲雾灵山
2116

山

滦

河

小五台山
2882▲

张家口

▲恒山

山海关

秦皇岛

北京

唐山

永

定

河

天津

保定

海

河

渤

海

030

牛河梁及红山文化重要遗址分布图

The locations and distribution of Niuheliang and
the important sites of Hongshan Culture

1.	赤峰市红山后	Hongshanhou
2.	翁牛特旗赛沁塔拉	Sanxingtala
3.	巴林右旗那斯台	Nasitai
4.	巴林左旗尖山子	Jianshanzi
5.	敖汉旗草帽山	Caomaoshan
6.	建平县五十家子	Wushijiazi
7.	围场县下伙房	Xiahuofang
8.	锦西县沙锅屯	Shaguotun
9.	喀左县东山嘴	Dongshanzui
10.	朝阳市牛河梁	Niuheliang
11.	阜新县胡头沟	Hutougou
12.	盘锦市郊	Suburbs of Panjin city
13.	康平县郊	Suburbs of Kangping county
14.	平鲁县坤都岭	Kunduling
15.	科左中旗新艾力	Xin'aili

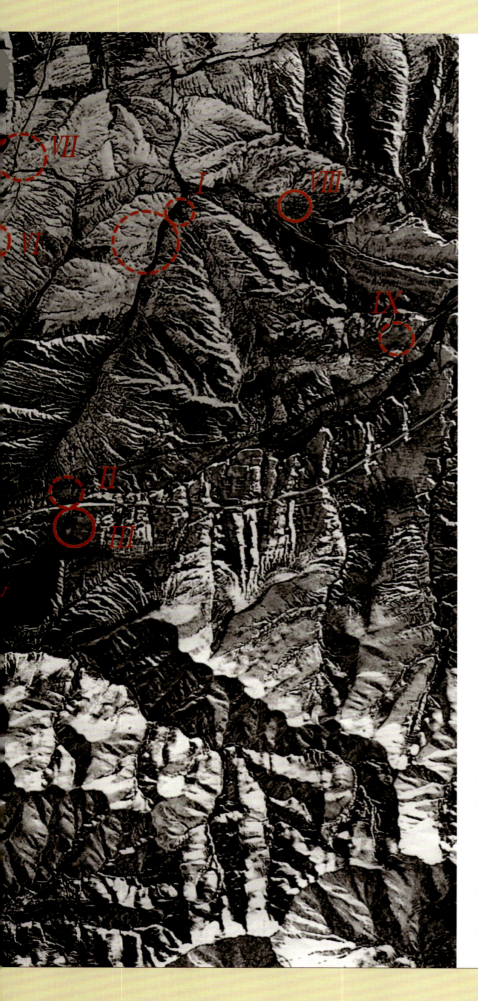

牛河梁遗址群总体布局图

General Distribution of Niuheliang
Sites Complex

Ⅰ 女神庙
The Goddes Temple

Ⅱ-Ⅻ ⅩⅣ-ⅩⅥ 积石冢
Stone mounds

ⅩⅢ 金字塔式巨形建筑遗址
Pyramid-shaped huge construction remains

1 考古发掘品
ARCHAEOLOGICAL FINDINGS

FUXIN, LIAONING PROVINCE

1. Jade *Jue* Ring
2. Jade *Jue* Ring
3. Cylindrical Jade *Jue* Ring
4. Dagger-shaped Jade
5. Dagger-shaped Jades
6. Fish-shaped Turquoise Ornaments
7. Three-ring Jade *Bi* Disc

FAKU, LIAONING PROVINCE

8. Jade Tortoise

KAZUO, LIAONING PROVINCE

9. Bird-shaped Turquoise Ornament
10. Jade *Huang* Semicircle in the Shape of Two Dragon Heads

JIANPING AND LINGYUAN, LIAONING PROVINCE

11. Jade Dragon
12. Jade Dragon
13. Hoof-shaped Jade
14. Hoof-shaped Jade
15. Jade in the Shape of Hook and Cloud
16. Jade in the Shape of Hook and Cloud
17. Jade Bead
18. Jade Bird
19. Jade *Bi* Disc
20. Jade *Bi* Disc
21. Jade Bracelet
22. Jade Ring
23. Jade Ring
24. Jade Ring
25. Comb Ornament with Two Beast Heads

26. Awl-shaped Jades
27. Stone *Yue* Battle-axe

AOHAN, INNER MONGOLIA AUTONOMOUS REGION

28. Stone Figure
29. Hoof-shaped Jade
30. Jade Arm Ornament
31. Jade *Bi* Disc
32. Jade Bird
33. Jade in the Shape of Hook and Cloud
34. Hook-shaped Jade

HEBEI PROVINCE

35. Jade Dragon

SHANXI PROVINCE

36. Jade *Bi* Disc

BEIPIAO, LIAONING PROVINCE

37. Jade Bird

HENAN PROVINCE

38. Jade in the Shape of Hook and Cloud
39. Hook-shaped Jade
40. Jade Dragon
41. Jade in the Shape of Hook and Cloud
42. Hoof-shaped Jade

SHAANXI PROVINCE

43. Jade Dragon
44. Jade Dragon
45. Jade in the Shape of Hook and Cloud

辽宁阜新

1. 玉玦
2. 玉玦
3. 柱状玉玦
4. 匕形玉器
5. 匕形玉器
6. 鱼形绿松石耳饰
7. 三联玉璧

辽宁法库

8. 玉龟

辽宁喀左

9. 绿松石鸟形饰
10. 双龙首玉璜

辽宁建平-凌源

11. 玉雕龙
12. 玉雕龙
13. 斜口筒形玉器
14. 斜口筒形玉器
15. 勾云形玉器
16. 勾云形玉器
17. 玉珠
18. 玉鸟
19. 玉璧
20. 玉璧
21. 玉镯
22. 玉环
23. 玉环
24. 玉环
25. 双兽首玉梳背饰

26. 棒锥形玉器
27. 石钺

内蒙古敖汉旗

28. 石雕人像
29. 斜口筒形玉器
30. 玉臂饰
31. 玉璧
32. 玉鸟
33. 勾云形玉器
34. 钩形玉器

河北

35. 玉雕龙

山西

36. 玉璧

辽宁北票

37. 玉鸟

河南

38. 勾云形玉器
39. 钩形玉器
40. 玉雕龙
41. 勾云形玉器
42. 斜口筒形玉器

陕西

43. 玉雕龙
44. 玉雕龙
45. 勾云形玉器

2 玉玦 （FCT0407②：6）

Jade *Jue* Ring

阜新查海遗址出土
现藏辽宁省文物考古研究所
直径 3.96、孔径 1.8、厚 1.22 厘米
Unearthed at Chahai site, Fuxin
Collection of Liaoning Provincial Institute of Cultural Relics
and Archaeology
Dia. 3.96 cm, (perforation) 1.8 cm; T. 1.22 cm
发表于《辽海文物学刊》1991 年 1 期，方殿春：《阜新查
海新石器时代遗址的初步发掘与分析》（线图见第 30 页图
三，1）。
乳白色，绿色以点状显现。环体，通体磨光，对钻孔。玦
口线切割，斜向切口，切面不平。

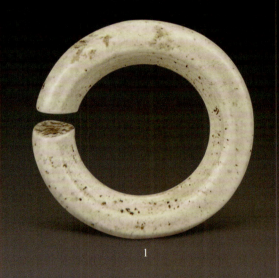

1

2

1 玉玦 （94FCTIF43：3）

Jade *Jue* Ring

阜新查海遗址出土
现藏辽宁省文物考古研究所
直径 3、孔径 1.78、厚 0.61 厘米
Unearthed at Chahai site, Fuxin
Collection of Liaoning Provincial Institute of Cultural
Relics and Archaeology
Dia. 3 cm, (perforation) 1.78 cm; T. 0.61 cm
发表于《中国文物报》1995 年 3 月 19 日。该文报
道了第 43 号房址内居室葬中随葬一对玉玦。
乳白色，通体磨光，体较细，环形，内孔缘起棱，
截面呈弧线三角形，玦口线切割，斜向切口，切面不齐。

4 匕形玉器（T0307②：1）

Dagger-shaped Jade

阜新查海遗址出土
现藏辽宁省文物考古研究所
长 11.6 厘米
Unearthed at Chahai site, Fuxin
Collection of Liaoning Provincial Institute of Cultural Relics
and Archaeology
L. 11.6 cm

发表于《辽海文物学刊》1991 年 1 期，方殿春：《阜新查海新石器时代遗址的初步发掘与分析》（线图见第 30 页图三，5）。

乳白色，显点状绿色。通体磨制。长条形，体内凹，壁薄而匀。顶端平，近顶端钻单孔，另端圆弧。这类匕形器与玉玦共出，是查海、兴隆洼文化玉器的一个基本组合，也见于日本海东岸的福井县桑野遗址和俄罗斯滨海洲，表现出东北亚广大地区间的文化联系。

3

3 柱状玉玦（T0505②：1）

Cylindrical Jade *Jue* Ring

阜新查海遗址出土
现藏辽宁省文物考古研究所
通高 1.95、最大直径 2.28、最小直径 2.05、内径 0.61 厘米
Unearthed at Chahai site, Fuxin
Collection of Liaoning Provincial Institute of Cultural Relics
and Archaeology
H. 1.95 cm; Dia. (max) 2.28 cm, (min) 2.05 cm, (inner) 0.61 cm

发表于《辽海文物学刊》1991 年 1 期，方殿春：《阜新查海新石器时代遗址的初步发掘与分析》（线图见第 30 页图三，2）。

乳白色，显点状绿色。整体作椭圆形柱状，通体磨光。对钻孔，玦口线切割，切口稍斜，切面不平。环状玉玦与柱状玉玦的组合，也见于江苏江阴祁头山马家浜等文化遗址，是玦类起源一元说的重要证据。

4

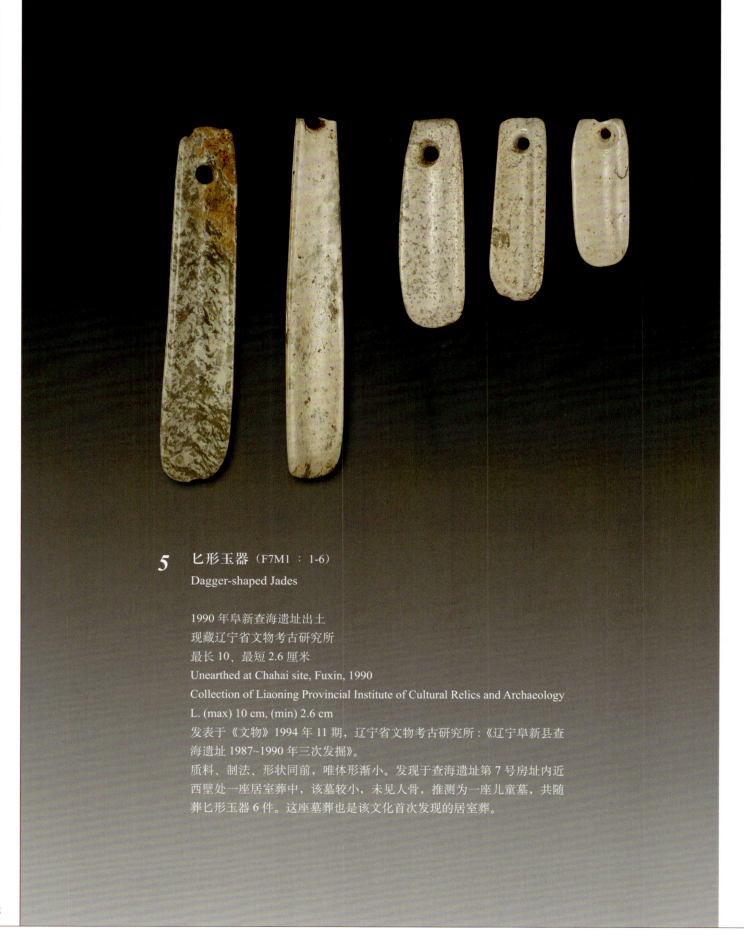

5 匕形玉器（F7M1：1-6）

Dagger-shaped Jades

1990 年阜新查海遗址出土

现藏辽宁省文物考古研究所

最长 10、最短 2.6 厘米

Unearthed at Chahai site, Fuxin, 1990

Collection of Liaoning Provincial Institute of Cultural Relics and Archaeology

L. (max) 10 cm, (min) 2.6 cm

发表于《文物》1994 年 11 期，辽宁省文物考古研究所：《辽宁阜新县查海遗址 1987~1990 年三次发掘》。

质料、制法、形状同前，唯体形渐小。发现于查海遗址第 7 号房址内近西壁处一座居室葬中，该墓较小，未见人骨，推测为一座儿童墓，共随葬匕形玉器 6 件。这座墓葬也是该文化首次发现的居室葬。

6 **鱼形绿松石耳饰**（胡M3-3:1、胡M3-5:1）

Fish-shaped Turquoise Ornaments

1973 年阜新胡头沟红山文化积石冢 3 号墓出土
现藏辽宁省博物馆
胡 M3-3:1 长 2.5 厘米
胡 M3-5:1 长 2.7 厘米
Unearthed from Tomb 3 of Hongshan Culture stone tombs at Hutougou, Fuxin, 1973
Collection of Museum of Liaoning Province
胡 M3-3: 1 L. 2.5 cm
胡 M3-5: 1 L. 2.7 cm

发表于《文物》1984 年 6 期，方殿春、刘葆华：《辽宁阜新县胡头沟红山文化玉器墓的发现》（线图见第 4 页图九，1、2）。

片状，表层为绿松石质，背层为一种黑色石皮。选择这种"两层皮"的绿松石料，是红山文化的一个特点，也偶见于其他史前文化，如陕西汉中龙岗寺第 314 号墓璜形饰等。

鱼的造型甚为简略，但有头、尾、鳍的明确表现，头部穿一孔成目，总体不显呆板。

两件质料相同，造型初看也相同，似为一对，但一件稍长，且鳍边起波线。此墓为多室墓，共隔为五室，至北而南分别编号为 1 ~ 5 室，此两件分别出于第 3 室和第 5 室，知其在使用上也并非一对，而是单耳坠。单耳坠的习俗，在牛河梁遗址也见于其他墓中，特别值得注意的是，牛河梁女神庙遗址所出女神头像，右耳完整耳垂部无穿孔，而左耳残缺，却在耳垂部残断处显示一孔，是单耳坠习俗的又一例，也是女神像仿真人塑造的实证。

7 三联玉璧（胡 M3 : 3）

Three-ring Jade *Bi* Disc

1973 年阜新胡头沟红山文化积石冢 3 号墓出土

现藏辽宁省博物馆

通高 6.4、最宽 3.15 厘米

Unearthed from Tomb 3 of Hongshan Culture stone tombs at Hutougou, Fuxin, 1973

Collection of Museum of Liaoning Province

H. 6.4 cm; W. (max) 3.15 cm

发表于《文物》1984 年 6 期，方殿春、刘葆华：《辽宁阜新县胡头沟红山文化玉器墓的发现》（线图见第 4 页图九，3）。

淡绿色玉，间红褐瑕斑，三璧垂直相连而成，三璧的外侧边似一条弧线，断以缺口，自上而下逐渐增大。下璧下圆上方，中璧扁方，上璧近圆三角形，上璧顶端内凹，与端面正中一凹槽相连。

多联璧是红山文化玉器特点之一，多见为二联璧和三联璧。东北地区史前文化也常有这类多联璧出土，有的如黑龙江省亚布力所出个体更大，且有的年代可能早于红山文化，故这类多联璧可视为东北地区史前玉器的一个共同地域特征。大汶口文化和长江下游诸考古文化偶有多联璧发现，一般认为是受到红山文化或东北史前文化影响。

8 玉龟 （铁考0453 0075）

Jade Tortoise

1978 年法库叶茂台西山第 19 号辽墓填土出土
现藏铁岭市博物馆
长 5.2、宽 3、最厚 1.7 厘米
Unearthed from Liao Tomb 19 at Qianxishan, Yemaotai, Faku, 1978
Collection of Tieling Museum, Liaoning Province
L. 5.2 cm; W. 3 cm; T. (max) 1.7 cm

表面灰白色，显绿色玉质地。龟形，龟体的前端窄而甚厚，后部宽而渐薄。吻部尖，口张，双圆凸目，颈部作前伸状。颈与龟体之间做出深凹槽，使细而长的颈部与龟体之间界限明显。背甲表面以甚浅的斜行条状纹显示甲壳结构，颈及肩部还刻有甚细的线纹。尖尾较长，尾端锐。背面斜平，背面中部遗有大块残凹坑。颈部横穿单孔，以一面钻为主。

玉龟在红山文化多有发现，且有龟有鳖，有龟形有龟壳。此玉龟的形态又有所不同，如头部五官刻划明显，体前厚后薄，背甲刻出似甲壳结构的纹饰等，表现为写实与神化更为巧妙的结合。

此标本出土于一辽代墓葬的填土中，同出有红山文化彩陶片和石核、石镞等细石器，与分布于附近的红山文化遗址有关。这一带近于辽河西岸，已是红山文化分布的东界。

1

辽宁喀左
KAZUO, LIAONING PROVINCE

9 绿松石鸟形饰（TC⑥2∶1）

Bird-shaped Turquoise Ornament

1982 年喀左东山嘴遗址出土
现藏辽宁省文物考古研究所
高 2.4、宽 2.8、厚 0.4 厘米
Unearthed at Dongshanzui site, Kazuo, 1982
Collection of Liaoning Provincial Institute of Cultural Relics and
Archaeology
H. 2.4 cm; W. 2.8 cm; T. 0.4 cm
发表于《文物》1984 年 11 期，郭大顺、张克举：《辽宁省喀左东
山嘴红山文化建筑群址发掘简报》（线图见第 9 页图一九，2）。
片状，分两层，作展翅形，正面用细线雕出头部、两翼及尾部，
背面为黑色，有一隧孔。此器为较薄的片状，有松石的一面更薄，
雕线需甚浅才可避免露出黑皮，此件雕纹不仅甚浅，且粗细均匀，
线条还十分流畅，更在饰纹中间磨出甚浅的瓦沟纹即打洼，工艺
技法堪称精到。

一

1

10 双龙首玉璜（TE6②g1∶1）

Jade *Huang* Semicircle in the Shape of Two Dragon Heads

1979 年喀左东山嘴遗址出土
现藏辽宁省文物考古研究所
长 4.1 厘米
Unearthed at Dongshanzui site, Kazuo, 1979
Collection of Liaoning Provincial Institute of Cultural Relics and
Archaeology
L. 4.1 cm

发表于《文物》1984 年 11 期，郭大顺、张克举：《辽宁省喀左县
东山嘴红山文化建筑群址发掘简报》（线图见第 9 页图一九，1）。
淡绿色，璜形，一面雕纹，另一面平面光素，只中部对穿一孔。
穿孔残。两端各作一龙首，吻前伸，上唇翘起，口微张，眼为菱
形框，身饰瓦沟纹。此器虽甚小，但龙首特征明确，是红山文化
龙形玉的第一次正式出土品。有以为形象近于甲骨文中的"虹"字，
那当是更为进步的造型。

11　玉雕龙（N2Z2M4：2）

Jade Dragon

1984 年建平牛河梁遗址第二地点一号冢 4 号墓出土
现藏辽宁省文物考古研究所
通高 10.3、宽 7.8、厚 3.3 厘米
Unearthed from Tomb 4, Complex 1, Locality 2 at
Niuheliang site, Jianping, 1984
Collection of Liaoning Provincial Institute of Cultural
Relics and Archaeology
H. 10.3 cm; W. 7.8 cm; T. 3.3 cm

发表于《文物》1986 年 6 期，辽宁省文物考古研究所：
《辽宁牛河梁红山文化"女神庙"与积石冢群发掘简
报》（线图见第 9 页图一一，1）。

淡绿色，微泛黄，通体精磨，光泽圆润。背及底部
有红褐色斑块，背面的斑块大，颜色尤重，且不够
光滑，疑为河磨玉的皮壳部分。龙体一侧也有白色
瑕斑，近耳部且有一道裂纹。龙体卷曲如环，头尾
切开又似玦。体扁圆而厚，环孔由两侧对钻，孔缘
经磨光，圆而光滑。背上部钻单孔，孔缘不够规则。
兽首形，短立耳较大，两耳之间从额中到头顶起短
棱脊。目圆而稍鼓，但圆度不够规则，吻部前凸，
有鼻孔，口略张开。前额与吻部刻多道阴线，吻部
五道，较深，鼻下两道，鼻上三道。

这是红山文化玉器中最具代表性的器类之一——玉
雕龙中的第一件正式考古发掘品，对红山文化玉器
时代的最终确定，起到"一锤定音"的作用。

1

12 玉雕龙（N2Z2M4：3）

Jade Dragon

1984 年建平牛河梁遗址第二地点一号冢 4 号墓出土
现藏中国国家博物馆
通高 7.9、宽 5.6、厚 2.5 厘米
Unearthed from Tomb 4, Complex 1, Locality 2 at Niuheliang site, Jianping, 1984
Collection of National Museum of China
H. 7.9 cm; W. 5.6 cm; T. 2.5 cm
发表于《文物》1986 年 6 期，辽宁省文物考古研究所：《辽宁牛河梁红山文化
"女神庙"与积石冢群发掘简报》（线图见第 9 页图一一，2）。
白色。形近标本 M4：2，唯体较小，头尾在环孔处相连。头部刻划的线条甚
为粗简，神态的表达也远不如标本 M4：2。出土时与 M4：2 玉雕龙相背而
置，应是作为一对来对待的，但此件不仅规格较小，而且质地、工艺都远不
及另一件，表现为对称中的不对称观念。而且此件质地较软却工艺较为粗简，
另一件质地甚硬，却工艺较精，这种选料和工艺上的反差，又表明当时对制
玉工艺掌握已达到得心应手的境界。

13 斜口筒形玉器（N2Z2M4：1）

Hoof-shaped Jade

1984 年建平牛河梁遗址第二地点一号冢 4 号墓出土

现藏辽宁省文物考古研究所

通高 18.6、平口长径 7.4、斜口最宽 10.7、壁厚 0.3~0.7 厘米

Unearthed from Tomb 4, Complex 1, Locality 2 at Niuheliang site, Jianping, 1984

Collection of Liaoning Provincial Institute of Cultural Relics and Archaeology

H. 18.6 cm; Dia. (non-slanting, long) 7.4 cm; W. (slanting, max) 10.7 cm; T. 0.3 − 0.7 cm

发表于《文物》1986 年 6 期，辽宁省文物考古研究所：《辽宁牛河梁红山文化"女神庙"与积石冢群发掘简报》(线图见第 9 页图一一,3)。深绿色玉，质匀，通体内外磨光，光泽圆润。扁圆筒状。一端作平口，一端作斜口。长面较平而宽，面上稍显内凹。斜口外敞，口缘磨薄似刃。平口两侧各钻一小孔，以由外向内钻为主。内壁及内壁上下边缘遗有用线切割法掏孔的痕迹，由短边中部为起点，向两侧切割，由左到右占大半圈，由右到左占小半圈。

斜口筒形玉器是红山文化玉器中出土数量较多的一类。此件为第一件正式考古发掘品，因出土位置枕于头下，多以为与束发有关，故称为"发箍"、"马蹄形玉箍"等，后知其出土位置不限于头部，也多见于腰部，且其基本特征如较宽一侧斜口、较窄一侧平口又穿孔等，与束发功能不合，故改称为"斜口筒形玉器"。2008 年发表安徽含山凌家滩 07M13 所出近似器为龟壳，受此启发，知斜口筒形玉器可能与龟壳有关，初步观察具龟壳特征的有：椭圆体、有长面与短面之分、边缘磨薄似刃；进一步观察：平口一端较窄，同于龟壳的前部，斜口一端较宽，同于龟壳的后部。此件出土时为原状态，平置，长面朝上，也为龟的正常状态；从内壁由中部分两次向两侧作线切割的明显痕迹，说明当时是作为两半来对待的；此外，史前时期所出龟壳多在背甲前部有对称钻孔，腹甲也有在前部正中钻孔的，都与斜口筒形玉器在平口两侧有对称钻孔相应。由于斜口筒形玉器有众多特征与龟壳相应，故可认为，斜口筒形玉器的原形，极有可能就是龟壳。

14 斜口筒形玉器（N16-79M2：4）

Hoof-shaped Jade

1979 年凌源牛河梁遗址第十六地点 2 号墓出土

现藏辽宁省博物馆

高 15.5、口径 5.8~7.4 厘米

Unearthed from Tomb 2, Locality 16 at Niuheliang site,
Lingyuan, 1979

Collection of Museum of Liaoning Province

H. 15.5 cm; Dia. 5.8 − 7.4 cm

发表于《考古》1986 年 6 期，李恭笃：《辽宁凌源县三官甸子城子山遗址试掘报告》。

青绿色，有大片白色瑕斑，间黑色斑点。磨制精。具斜口筒形玉器共同特点：器体扁圆，一端平口较窄，另端斜口较宽，形成由细而粗的筒状。器体规整，器壁薄厚较匀，内外壁平直光滑，斜口部分尤为规整。不过在腹壁内侧上部仍遗有掏芯时的钻程痕。近平口的两端边各有一对钻小孔，以单面钻为主。

1

15 勾云形玉器 （N16-79M2：1）

Jade in the Shape of Hook and Cloud

1979 年凌源牛河梁遗址第十六地点 2 号墓出土

现藏辽宁省博物馆

长 22.5、宽 11.2、厚 0.8 厘米

Unearthed from Tomb 2, Locality 16 at Niuheliang site, Lingyuan, 1979

Collection of Museum of Liaoning Province

L. 22.5 cm; W. 11.2 cm; T. 0.8 cm

发表于《考古》1986 年 6 期，李恭笃：《辽宁凌源县三官甸子城子山遗址试掘报告》。

淡绿色玉。板状，器体呈长方形，由中部与四角的卷勾组成。正面打洼，在与卷勾走向相同的部位琢磨出浅凹槽纹。背面平整，分布有四组隧孔，隧孔都与短边平行，并在钻孔前先钻沟槽，沟槽与长边平行。

勾云形玉器是红山文化玉器中又一代表性器类，此件为首次正式发掘品。为单勾形，有正、背之分，勾云形玉器的出土状态都为竖置，此件为斜置，不过从背面隧孔与长面为垂直方向看，仍是以竖行为正常置法。

16 勾云形玉器（N2Z2M9：2）

Jade in the Shape of Hook and Cloud

1984 年建平牛河梁遗址第二地点 1 号冢 9 号墓出土

现藏辽宁省文物考古研究所

长 6.2、宽 2.4、厚 0.4 厘米

Unearthed from Tomb 9, Complex 1, Locality 2 at Niuheliang site, Jianping, 1984

Collection of Liaoning Provincial Institute of Cultural Relics and Archaeology

L. 6.2 cm; W. 2.4 cm; T. 0.4 cm

发表于《中国文物考古之美·1》（图版 34），文物出版社／（台）光复书局，1994 年。

淡绿色玉、圆润光泽。为简化勾云形玉器，体面平而无纹饰，仅在卷勾处稍有加工。底缘有三组 6 枚齿状突。体中部对钻双孔，上缘中部对穿单孔。此件简化型玉器所在的墓葬位置在冢的最南边，是否为晚期形制，有待进一步证据。

1

17 玉珠（N167-9M2：7）
Jade Bead

1979 年凌源牛河梁遗址第十六地点 2 号墓出土
现藏辽宁省博物馆
高 1.1、宽 1.1、直径 1.4、孔径 0.4 厘米
Unearthed from Tomb 2, Locality 16 at Niuheliang site, Lingyuan, 1979
Collection of Museum of Liaoning Province
H. 1.1 cm; W. 1.1 cm; Dia. 1.4 cm, (perforation) 0.4 cm
发表于《考古》1986 年 6 期，李恭笃：《辽宁凌源县三官甸子城子
山遗址试掘报告》（线图见第 501 页图八，3）。
淡绿色，质匀，有白色瑕斑。精磨，光泽细腻。器体呈亚腰柱状，
近椭圆形，中部有对钻长孔，两端面稍内凹。
玉珠是红山文化玉器中较为常见的玉类，出土时置于墓主胸部，虽
无其他串珠一类相配，也可推测为项饰一类，但红山文化玉珠不同
于一般珠类，个体较大，选料较精，且作束腰，凹面，精磨，制作
较为费工，是为较重要的玉类。

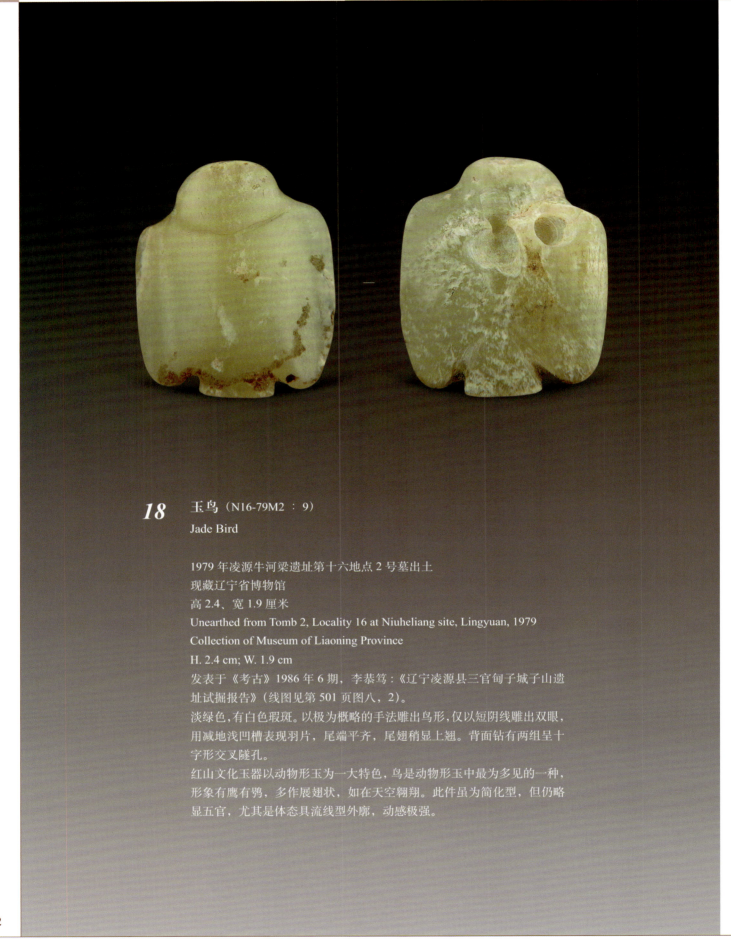

18 玉鸟（N16-79M2：9）

Jade Bird

1979 年凌源牛河梁遗址第十六地点 2 号墓出土

现藏辽宁省博物馆

高 2.4、宽 1.9 厘米

Unearthed from Tomb 2, Locality 16 at Niuheliang site, Lingyuan, 1979

Collection of Museum of Liaoning Province

H. 2.4 cm; W. 1.9 cm

发表于《考古》1986 年 6 期，李恭笃：《辽宁凌源县三官甸子城子山遗址试掘报告》（线图见第 501 页图八，2）。

淡绿色，有白色瑕斑。以极为概略的手法雕出鸟形，仅以短阴线雕出双眼，用减地浅凹槽表现羽片，尾端平齐，尾翅稍显上翘。背面钻有两组呈十字形交叉隧孔。

红山文化玉器以动物形玉为一大特色，鸟是动物形玉中最为多见的一种，形象有鹰有鸮，多作展翅状，如在天空翱翔。此件虽为简化型，但仍略显五官，尤其是体态具流线型外廓，动感极强。

1

19　玉璧（N16-79M2 ： 5）

Jade *Bi* Disc

1979 年凌源牛河梁遗址第十六地点 2 号墓出土

现藏辽宁省博物馆

外缘边长 10.1~11.5、内缘直径 2.5、厚 0.7 厘米

Unearthed from Tomb 2, Locality 16 at Niuheliang site, Lingyuan, 1979

Collection of Museum of Liaoning Province

Periphery (outer) 10.1 － 11.5 cm; Dia. (inner) 2.5 cm; T. 0.7 cm

发表于《考古》1986 年 6 期，李恭笃：《辽宁凌源县三官甸子城子
山遗址试掘报告》（线图见第 501 页图七，1）。

淡黄色，间白色瑕斑。内缘呈正圆形，外廓近于方形。上部较宽，
四边稍显外弧，四角圆。内外缘磨薄似刃，靠近一侧边缘正中并排
对钻两个小圆孔，以单面钻为主。

20 玉璧（N16-79M2：6）

Jade *Bi* Disc

1979 年凌源牛河梁遗址第十六地点 2 号墓出土

现藏辽宁省博物馆

外缘边长 10.2~12.7、内缘直径 3.2、厚 0.5 厘米

Unearthed from Tomb 2, Locality 16 at Niuheliang site, Lingyuan, 1979

Collection of Museum of Liaoning Province

Periphery (outer) 10.2 − 12.7 cm; Dia. (inner) 3.2 cm; T. 0.5 cm

发表于《考古》1986 年 6 期，李恭笃：《辽宁凌源县三官甸子城子山遗址试掘报告》。

青绿色，有大片白色瑕斑。外缘为方形圆角，内缘为不规则的圆形。边缘磨薄似刃。靠近外缘一侧边正中对钻一个小圆孔。

红山文化的玉璧，以内孔缘圆、外缘方圆、壁面中鼓、边缘薄似刃为主要特点，此件外缘更近于方形。

1

21 **玉镯**（N16-79M2：3）

Jade Bracelet

1979 年凌源牛河梁遗址第十六地点 2 号墓出土
现藏辽宁省博物馆
直径 8、孔径 6.3、厚 0.8 厘米
Unearthed from Tomb 2, Locality 16 at Niuheliang site, Lingyuan, 1979
Collection of Museum of Liaoning Province
Dia. 8 cm, (perforation) 6.3 cm; T. 0.8 cm
发表于《考古》1986 年 6 期，李恭笃：《辽宁凌源县三官甸子城子
山遗址试掘报告》（线图见第 501 页图八，2）。
淡绿色，质匀无瑕。镯体近正圆形，内缘面平，外缘起棱，横截面
呈三角形。
红山文化的玉环与玉镯较为多见，出土时有置或套于手腕的为镯，
另置者为环，镯体虽简，佩戴于外，要求色泽纯净，用料亦大，是
红山文化玉器中又一重要玉类。

22　玉环（N2Z2M1：1）

Jade Ring

1981 年建平牛河梁遗址第二地点一号冢 1 号墓出土
现藏辽宁省文物考古研究所
直径 11、孔径 9 厘米

Unearthed from Tomb 1, Complex 1, Locality 2 at
Niuheliang site, Jianping, 1981
Collection of Liaoning Provincial Institute of Cultural
Relics and Archaeology
Dia. 11 cm, (perforation) 9 cm

发表于《文物》1984 年 6 期，孙守道、郭大顺：《论
辽河流域的原始文明与龙的起源》（墓葬图片见第
13 页图二）。

白色蛇纹岩质。正圆形，环面精磨，近外环缘磨薄，
使外环缘起棱锐，环体的横截面呈锐三角形。环体
一孔，为两面对钻而成。内缘大孔为管钻，内孔缘
尚保留管钻遗留痕迹，可见斜直的壁缘和内孔壁上
下边缘所遗甚锐的边棱，其中一侧边棱还有明显的
断痕，应是钻孔未尽敲击剥离内芯时所致。

这是红山文化玉器确认过程中第一个正式发掘品，
而且因为此器内缘保留的管钻痕迹甚为明显，孔径
又大，表明当时已掌握了用直径达 9 厘米的大口径
钻管进行管钻的技术。此环出土位置在头顶部左侧，
为这类玉环的功能解读提供了新线索。

23

23 玉环（N16-79M2：2）

Jade Ring

1979 年凌源牛河梁遗址第十六地点 2 号墓出土
现藏辽宁省博物馆
直径 6.25、孔径 5.3、厚 0.4 厘米
Unearthed from Tomb 2, Locality 16 at Niuheliang site,
Lingyuan, 1979
Collection of Museum of Liaoning Province
Dia. 6.25 cm, (perforation) 5.3 cm; T. 0.4 cm
发表于《考古》1986 年 6 期，李恭笃：《辽宁凌源
县三官甸子城子山遗址试掘报告》（线图见第 501 页
图七，3）。
淡绿色，有白色瑕斑。出土于墓主胸部。内缘面较平，
外缘起棱，横截面呈三角形。

24 玉环（N16-79M2：8）

Jade Ring

1979 年凌源牛河梁遗址第十六地点 2 号墓出土
现藏辽宁省博物馆
直径 6.4、孔径 5.4、厚 0.4 厘米
Unearthed from Tomb 2, Locality 16 at Niuheliang site,
Lingyuan, 1979
Collection of Museum of Liaoning Province
Dia. 6.4 cm, (perforation) 5.4 cm; T. 0.4 cm
发表于《考古》1986 年 6 期，李恭笃：《辽宁凌源
县三官甸子城子山遗址试掘报告》（线图见第 501 页
图七，3）。
淡绿色，有白色瑕斑。形制与 N1679M2：2 相近。
出土于墓主右脚部。

1

24

25 双兽首玉梳背饰（N16-79M1：4）

Comb Ornament with Two Beast Heads

1979 年凌源牛河梁遗址第十六地点 3 号墓西侧扰土中出土

现藏辽宁省博物馆

高 2.6、长 8.9、宽 1.8、孔径 1.9 厘米

Unearthed west of Tomb 3, Locality 16 at Niuheliang site, Lingyuan, 1979

Collection of Museum of Liaoning Province

H. 2.6 cm; L. 8.9 cm; W. 1.8 cm; Dia. (perforation) 1.9 cm

发表于辽宁省文物考古研究所编著：《牛河梁——红山文化遗址发掘报告》（1983—2003 年度）中册（第 415 页 N16 图八二）、下册（图版二八四、二八五，1）文物出版社，2012 年。原编号为采 :2。

青白色，杂有较大面积黑斑。器体横长，两端各圆雕一兽首。兽首的额顶隆起，面廓近于三角形，耳呈圆弧状斜立，眼眶用减地凸起的菱形纹表示，吻部窄且略有上翘，特征似熊首。器身有与兽首大小相近的并列三大孔，使上部顶面呈三联弧状，下部底面则平直，底面近边缘处钻有四个与三圆孔相通的小圆孔，小圆孔每俩俩居于一侧，以单面钻为主，略呈漏斗形。器体还依兽首形状也呈上宽下窄状，近底处尤窄似榫，并在榫面阴刻一行平行短斜线纹。

这类三孔器在红山文化已发现有多例，底边都设有榫部，榫面上有成排穿孔，属复合器。随着浙江海盐周家滨良渚文化第 30 号墓玉梳背饰的正式出土，可知红山文化这类三孔器也应为玉梳背饰，牛河梁遗址第二地点一号冢第 17 号墓三孔器出土位置在头下是进一步证明。这类三孔器的两端均有装饰形象，此件两端所饰为动物头部，以圆雕手法雕出，非抽象而为写实型，由基本特征可确定为熊首。而且首部尺寸虽然较小，从整体轮廓到细部如耳、目、嘴却都有清楚而准确的交代，而且强调了两端熊首的差异。红山文化玉器中有属于圆雕的器物，如玉雕龙的首部，但多高度抽象，既为圆雕又写实的极少，所以这件圆雕作品十分珍贵。此外，这件玉器用料非红山文化常见的泛黄的淡绿色玉，而为灰白色间大块黑斑的玉料，一端熊头的半侧被黑色斑痕覆盖，另一端黑斑则出现在熊头的额部和吻部，作为一件讲究写实形象又十分费工的圆雕作品，选料如此独特，是值得注意的。

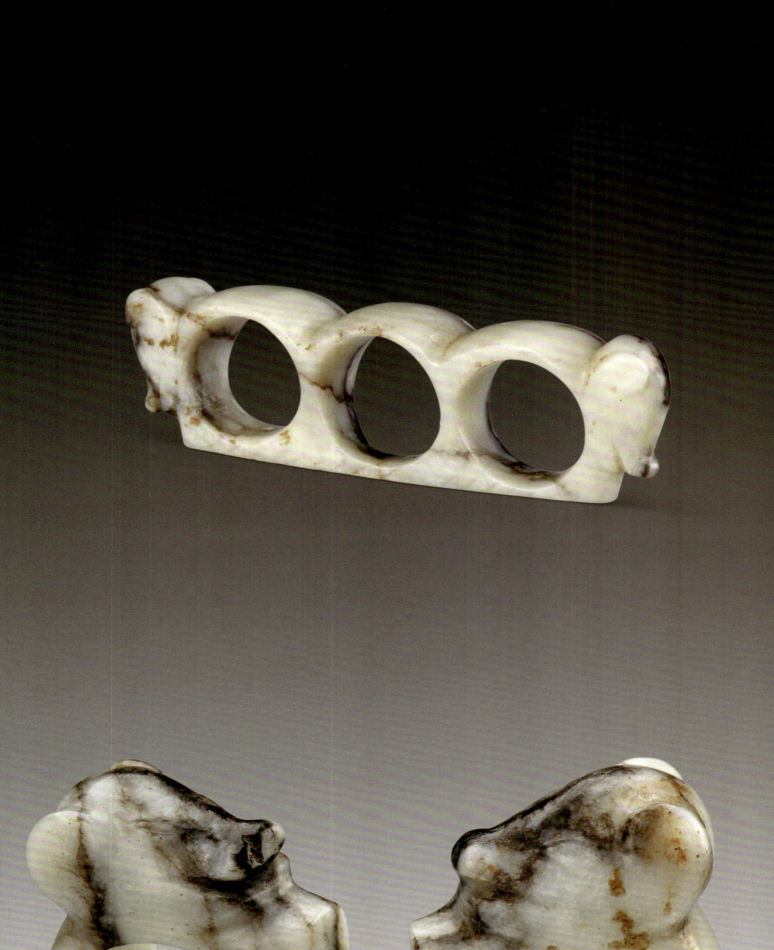

26 棒锥形玉器
(N16-79M1：1、N16-79M1：2、N16-79M1：3)

Awl-shaped Jades

1979 年凌源牛河梁遗址第十六地点 1 号墓出土
现藏朝阳市博物馆
N1679M1：1 长 15.5、粗端直径 1.4 厘米
N1679M1：2 长 14.8、粗端直径 1.5 厘米
N1679M1：3 长 22.6、粗端直径 2.1 厘米
Unearthed from Tomb 1, Locality 16 at Niuheliang site,
Lingyuan, 1979
Collection of Chaoyang Museum
N1679M1: 1 L. 15.5 cm; Dia. (max) 1.4 cm
N1679M1: 2 L. 14.8 cm; Dia. (max) 1.5 cm
N1679M1: 3 L. 22.6 cm; Dia. (max) 2.1 cm
发表于《考古》1986 年 6 期，李恭笃：《辽宁凌源县三官
甸子城子山遗址试掘报告》(墓葬线图见第 499 页图五)。
白色蛇纹岩质，局部见土渍痕，形制完全相同。
N1679M1：1 出土于墓主腰部左侧。器体呈细长柱状，
顶端作椭圆形微凸面，以下渐细，尾端呈圆尖状，尖部锋
利。横截面呈扁圆形，通体抛光；N1679M1：2 亦出土
于墓主腰部左侧，在 N1679M1：1 的内侧，质地、形制
与其相同，唯稍短；N1679M1：3 出土于墓葬的西侧扰
土中，原报告编号为采：3，质地、形制与 N1679M1：2
相同，唯稍长。

27 石钺（N2Z2M9：1）

Stone *Yue* Battle-axe

1984 年建平牛河梁遗址第二地点 1 号冢 9 号墓出土
现藏辽宁省文物考古研究所
长 11.6、宽 8.4、厚 1.4 厘米
Unearthed from Tomb 9, Complex 1, Locality 2 at Niuheliang site, Jianping, 1984
Collection of Liaoning Provincial Institute of Cultural Relics and Archaeology
L. 11.6 cm; W. 8.4 cm; T. 1.4 cm
发表于《玉魂国魄——红山文化玉器精品展》（第 80 页图版 66），浙江古籍出版社，2009 年。

砂岩质，灰色。体扁平。两侧边外弧，圆弧刃。顶面磨平，钺体一对钻单孔。这种宽体、圆弧刃、侧边外弧的形制，也见于大约同时期的其他史前文化，如江浙地区的崧泽文化，具共同的时代特征。

1

28　石雕人像

Stone Figure

敖汉旗草帽山第二地点积石冢出土

现藏敖汉旗博物馆

残高 18、头部高约 16 厘米

Unearthed from stone tombs at Locality 2, Caomaoshan, Aohan

Collection of Aohan Banner Museum

H. (fragment) 18 cm, (head) c. 16 cm

发表于《中国文物报》2001 年 8 月 29 日收藏鉴赏周刊 33 期《敖汉旗发现红山时代石雕神像》。

红砂岩质，出土于冢的中心部位（冢内方形石框北墙处散落的石堆下）。为圆雕。大体相当于真人的五分之二，人像表面较为粗糙，但雕造却十分讲究：面部较长，五官清晰，目微闭，有精心雕作的清晰的眼球轮廓。嘴也微闭。宽鼻梁，圆鼻头。最使人感到意外的，是在头部有结构十分明确而规整的冠饰，冠饰分两部分，一为头顶正中部位的弯板状冠饰，一为环绕额部一周的带状发箍。弯板状冠饰从前额弯向后部，与额上的带状发箍前后相连。冠饰的弯板形甚为宽厚，占据了头顶的大部分，是为冠饰的主体。已知牛河梁女神庙遗址曾发现大型泥塑人像，石雕大型人像也有线索，此件为正式发掘品，对认识红山文化雕塑艺术特别是石雕工艺又有新认识。这尊石雕人像，从头顶到面部的每道工序雕造的都很到位，一丝没有显出草率。各部位的比例也甚为恰当，所要表达的是一种安详而不张扬的神态。从颈部以下残缺情况可推测应为全身像。说明红山文化包括大型人像在内的石雕工艺，也已达到高度发达的水平。

29 斜口筒形玉器（NADM833：2）
Hoof-shaped Jade

敖汉旗大甸子夏家店下层文化 833 号墓出土
现藏中国社会科学院考古研究所
高 14、内径长径 6.4、内短径 4.4、壁最厚 0.4 厘米
Unearthed from Xiajiadian Lower Culture Tomb 833 at Dadianzi, Aohan
Collection of Institute of Archaeology, Chinese Academy of Social Sciences
H. 14 cm; Dia. (inner) (long) 6.4 cm, (short) 4.4 cm; T. (max) 0.4 cm
发表于中国社会科学院考古研究所编著：《大甸子——夏家店下层文化遗址与
墓地发掘报告》（第 174 页图八三，6），科学出版社，1998 年。
出土位置在腰间，横置，与人的脊椎相垂直。色偏黄，微泛红。内外壁磨光较
精。横截面为椭圆形。长筒状，一端斜口，一端平口。筒内侧有磨制加工痕迹，
斜口边缘有磨损痕。具红山文化斜口筒形玉器共同特点，唯近平口边无钻孔。
红山文化斜口筒形玉器出土位置以头部为多，但也有部分是置于腰间的，此件
不仅器类属红山文化，而且也置于腰间，可见传承之密切。

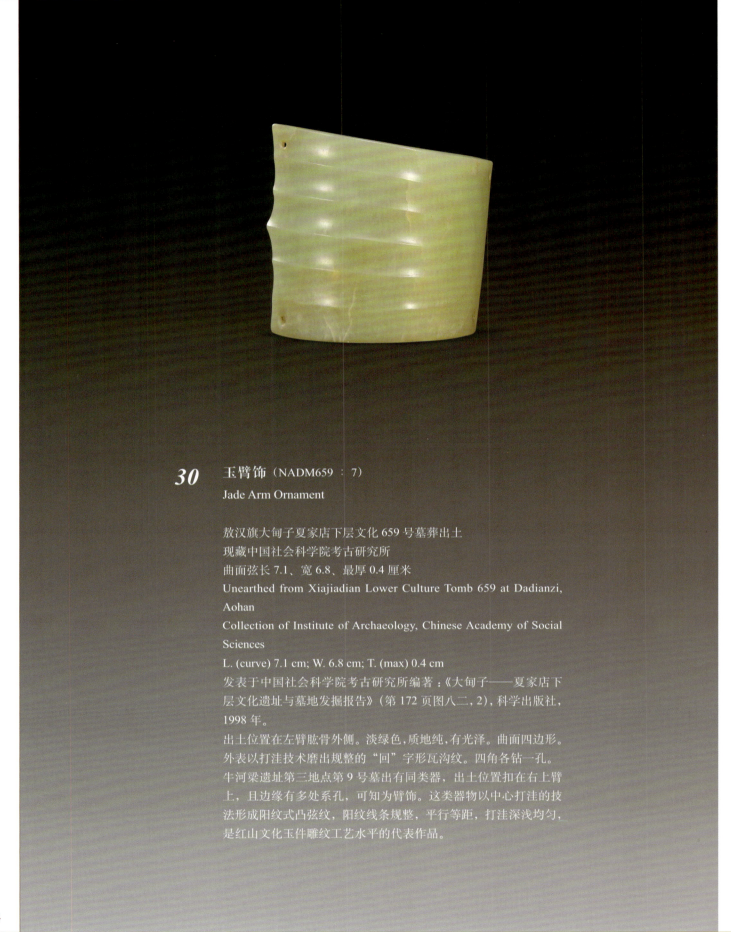

30 玉臂饰（NADM659 ： 7）

Jade Arm Ornament

敖汉旗大甸子夏家店下层文化 659 号墓葬出土
现藏中国社会科学院考古研究所
曲面弦长 7.1、宽 6.8、最厚 0.4 厘米
Unearthed from Xiajiadian Lower Culture Tomb 659 at Dadianzi,
Aohan
Collection of Institute of Archaeology, Chinese Academy of Social
Sciences
L. (curve) 7.1 cm; W. 6.8 cm; T. (max) 0.4 cm
发表于中国社会科学院考古研究所编著：《大甸子——夏家店下
层文化遗址与墓地发掘报告》（第 172 页图八二，2），科学出版社，
1998 年。
出土位置在左臂肱骨外侧。淡绿色，质地纯，有光泽。曲面四边形。
外表以打洼技术磨出规整的 "回" 字形瓦沟纹。四角各钻一孔。
牛河梁遗址第三地点第 9 号墓出有同类器，出土位置扣在右上臂
上，且边缘有多处系孔，可知为臂饰。这类器物以中心打洼的技
法形成阳纹式凸弦纹，阳纹线条规整，平行等距，打洼深浅均匀，
是红山文化玉件雕纹工艺水平的代表作品。

31 玉璧（NADM853:13）

Jade *Bi* Disc

敖汉旗大甸子夏家店下层文化 853 号墓出土

现藏中国社会科学院考古研究所

外径 8.2、内径 3.2、厚 0.4 厘米

Unearthed from Xiajiadian Lower Culture Tomb 853 at Dadianzi, Aohan

Collection of Institute of Archaeology, Chinese Academy of Social Sciences

Dia. (outer) 8.2 cm, (inner) 3.2 cm; T. 0.4 cm

发表于中国社会科学院考古研究所编著：《大甸子——夏家店下层文化遗址与墓地发掘报告》（第 170 页图八一，5），科学出版社，1998 年。

淡绿色，泛黄，有大片浅红色瑕斑。外缘不正圆，内缘圆，内外缘磨薄似刃，璧体中部较厚而鼓，这些都为红山文化玉璧特征。近外缘钻双孔，孔缘有系缚磨痕，故报告称为"璧形坠"。

32 玉鸟（NADM1257:4）

Jade Bird

敖汉旗大甸子夏家店下层文化 1257 号墓出土
现藏中国社会科学院考古研究所
长 3、宽 2、厚 0.5 厘米
Unearthed from Xiajiadian Lower Culture Tomb 1257 at Dadianzi, Aohan
L. 3 cm; W. 2 cm; T. 0.5 cm
发表于中国社会科学院考古研究所编著：《大甸子——夏家店下层文
化遗址与墓地发掘报告》（线图见第 174 页图八三，15，图版五四，1），
科学出版社，1998 年。报告称"雕花坠"。
墨绿色。形小。近于椭圆状，为鸟张翼的简化形式，体面平，首部、
羽翅与尾部的边缘雕有较粗的阴线。中心偏一侧钻一孔。

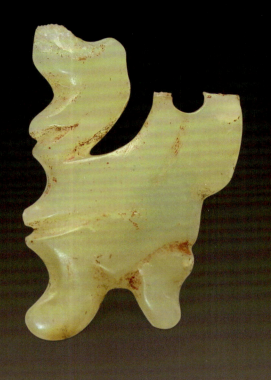

1

33　勾云形玉器（NADM373:7）

Jade in the Shape of Hook and Cloud

敖汉旗大甸子夏家店下层文化 373 号墓葬出土
现藏中国社会科学院考古研究所
残长 2.75、宽 1.7、厚 0.25 厘米
Unearthed from Xiajiadian Lower Culture Tomb 373 at Dadianzi, Aohan
Collection of Institute of Archaeology, Chinese Academy of Social Sciences
L. (fragment) 2.75 cm; W. 1.7 cm; T. 0.25 cm
发表于中国社会科学院考古研究所编著：《大甸子——夏家店下层文化
遗址与墓地发掘报告》（图版五二，2），科学出版社，1998 年。报告称
"镂花坠"。
出土位置在人胸部。黄绿色，较淡。近半残缺。形较小。边缘卷勾端圆
而不尖。器体打注较浅，边缘刻纹较深。长侧一边正中钻孔较大。值得
注意的是刻纹内有朱红色料遗留。

34　钩形玉器（NADM308∶1）
Hook-shaped Jade

敖汉旗大甸子夏家店下层文化 308 号墓出土
现藏中国社会科学院考古研究所
通长 7.1、宽 2.5、厚 0.7 厘米
Unearthed from Xiajiadian Lower Culture Tomb 308 at Dadianzi, Aohan
Collection of Institute of Archaeology, Chinese Academy of Social Sciences
L. 7.1 cm; W. 2.5 cm; T. 0.7 cm
发表于中国社会科学院考古研究所编著：《大甸子——夏家店下层文化遗址与
墓地发掘报告》（第 174 页图八三,5），科学出版社，1998 年。报告称"雕花坠"。
绿色。长条状玉片。一端卷曲似勾云形玉器一角，另端有短柄，柄端磨薄为榫，
榫部较大，榫端圆，榫面钻单孔，孔也较大。卷体与柄之间以双棱组成的栏相
隔。边缘与两面碾刻甚浅。
钩形器在红山文化玉器中都为收集品，尚无正式出土实例，此件虽出土于夏家
店下层文化墓葬中，但仍是迄今为止这种器类唯一一件正式考古发掘品。

35　**玉雕龙**（姜家梁墓75：1）
Jade Dragon

1995、1998 年河北阳原姜家梁遗址第 75 号墓出土
现藏河北省文物研究所
高 3.3、宽 2.6 厘米
Unearthed from Tomb 75 at Jiangjialiang site, Yangyuan,
Hebei Province, 1995 and 1998
Collection of Cultural Relics Institute of Hebei Province
H. 3.3 cm; W. 2.6 cm

发表于河北省文物研究所：《河北阳原姜家梁新石器时代遗址的
发掘》《考古》2001 年 2 期（第 23 页图二〇，8）。

乳白色。有裂纹。猪首，双耳高耸，吻前伸，鼻间有阴刻皱纹。
体卷曲，首尾相对，其外侧有缺口，内侧相连接。中部对钻大孔，
耳后有一对钻的小穿孔。制作精细，形象美观。姜家梁墓地属小
河沿文化，所出玉雕龙，质地约为白色蛇纹岩质，切口相连，头
部较大，雕纹甚简，应为流传到小河沿文化的一件红山文化玉器。

山西
SHANXI PROVINCE

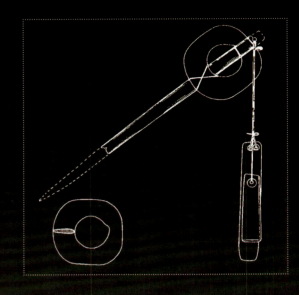

36 玉璧（M2036:1）

Jade *Bi* Disc

襄汾陶寺墓地出土
现藏中国社会科学院考古研究所
外周长径 4.8、短径 4.4、直径 2.1~2.35、厚 0.3 厘米
Unearthed at Taosi burial ground, Xiangfen
Collection of Institute of Archaeology, Chinese Academy of Social
Sciences
Dia. (outer) (long) 4.8 cm, (short) 4.4 cm; W. (disc) 2.1-2.35 cm; T. 0.3 cm
发表于（台）《海峡两岸古玉学会议论文专辑（1）》，高炜：《龙山时
代玉骨组合头饰的复原研究》（第 325 页图六，1），台湾大学理学院
地质科学系印行，2001 年。
为头饰的组成部分。有骨笄顶端由璧孔穿过，再以骨笄顶端的穿孔系
以长条状玉坠。玉璧内孔缘为不够规则的圆形，外缘为方圆形，内外
边缘薄似刃，最鼓处在近于内孔缘处，发掘者推定属红山文化玉器。

1

37　玉鸟（T8 ③：2）
　　　Jade Bird

1972 年北票丰下遗址出土
现藏辽宁省文物考古研究所
残高 3、宽 3、厚 0．6 厘米
Unearthed at Fengxia site, Beipiao, 1972
Collection of Liaoning Provincial Institute of Cultural Relics and Archaeology
H. (fragment) 3 cm; W. 3 cm; T. 0.6 cm
发表于《考古》1976 年 3 期，辽宁省文物干部培训班：《辽宁北票丰下遗址 1972 年春发掘简报》（线图见第 208 页图一六，1）。
深绿色，展翅鸟形，顶部穿单孔，正面两侧以减地阳纹表现羽翅。背面平而光素。下部一侧有残。
丰下遗址作为一处小型的夏家店下层文化遗址，也有红山文化玉器出土，可见红山文化玉器在夏家店下层文化中流传具有一定普遍性。

河南
HENAN PROVINCE

38 勾云形玉器（妇好墓 编号948）

Jade in the Shape of Hook and Cloud

1976 年安阳小屯村商代妇好墓出土
现藏中国社会科学院考古研究所
长 6.2、宽 1.9、厚 0.4 厘米
Unearthed from Shang tomb of Fu Hao at Xiaotun, Anyang,
Henan Province, 1976
Collection of Institute of Archaeology, Chinese Academy of
Social Sciences
L. 6.2 cm; W. 1.9 cm; T. 0.4 cm
发表于中国社会科学院考古研究所编：《殷墟妇好墓》（图
版一六，二下左），文物出版社，1980 年。
淡绿色，有褐斑。简化型。发掘报告称为"椭长形饰"。
两端为弧形，上侧近平，中部有一小豁口，两侧各有一小
孔，下侧有三个内凹的弧形缺口，可佩戴。

1

39 钩形玉器（妇好墓 编号964）

Hook-shaped Jade

1976 年安阳小屯村商代妇好墓出土
现藏于中国社会科学院考古研究所
长 9.1、后段宽 1.9、厚 0.5 厘米
Unearthed from Shang tomb of Fu Hao at Xiaotun, Anyang, Henan Province,
1976
Collection of Institute of Archaeology, Chinese Academy of Social Sciences
L. 9.1 cm; W. (end) 1.9 cm; T. 0.5 cm
发表于中国社会科学院考古研究所编：《殷墟妇好墓》（图九五，6；图
版一六四），文物出版社，1980 年。
黄绿色。有栏有榫，发掘报告称为"柄形器"。前段较直，薄榫上有圆孔，
后段呈弧形略下弯，似钩，中部较宽，有一条竖直浅槽。

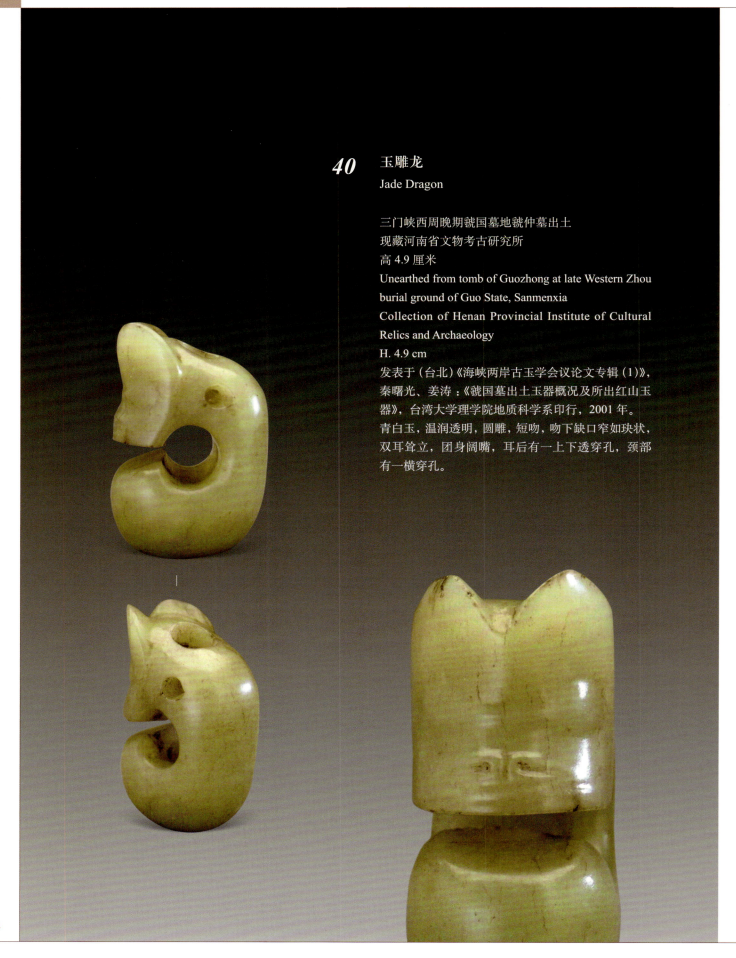

40 玉雕龙

Jade Dragon

三门峡西周晚期虢国墓地虢仲墓出土
现藏河南省文物考古研究所
高 4.9 厘米
Unearthed from tomb of Guozhong at late Western Zhou
burial ground of Guo State, Sanmenxia
Collection of Henan Provincial Institute of Cultural
Relics and Archaeology
H. 4.9 cm
发表于（台北）《海峡两岸古玉学会议论文专辑（1）》，
秦曙光、姜涛：《虢国墓出土玉器概况及所出红山玉
器》，台湾大学理学院地质科学系印行，2001 年。
青白玉，温润透明，圆雕，短吻，吻下缺口窄如玦状，
双耳耸立，团身阔嘴，耳后有一上下透穿孔，颈部
有一横穿孔。

41 勾云形玉器

Jade in the Shape of Hook and Cloud

三门峡西周晚期虢国墓地出土
现藏河南省文物考古研究所
高约 7 厘米
Unearthed at late Western Zhou burial ground of
Guo State, Sanmenxia
Collection of Henan Provincial Institute of Cultural
Relics and Archaeology
H.7 cm

为残件，似变形勾云形玉器。一侧残断处有穿孔，一端穿孔似经再加工。

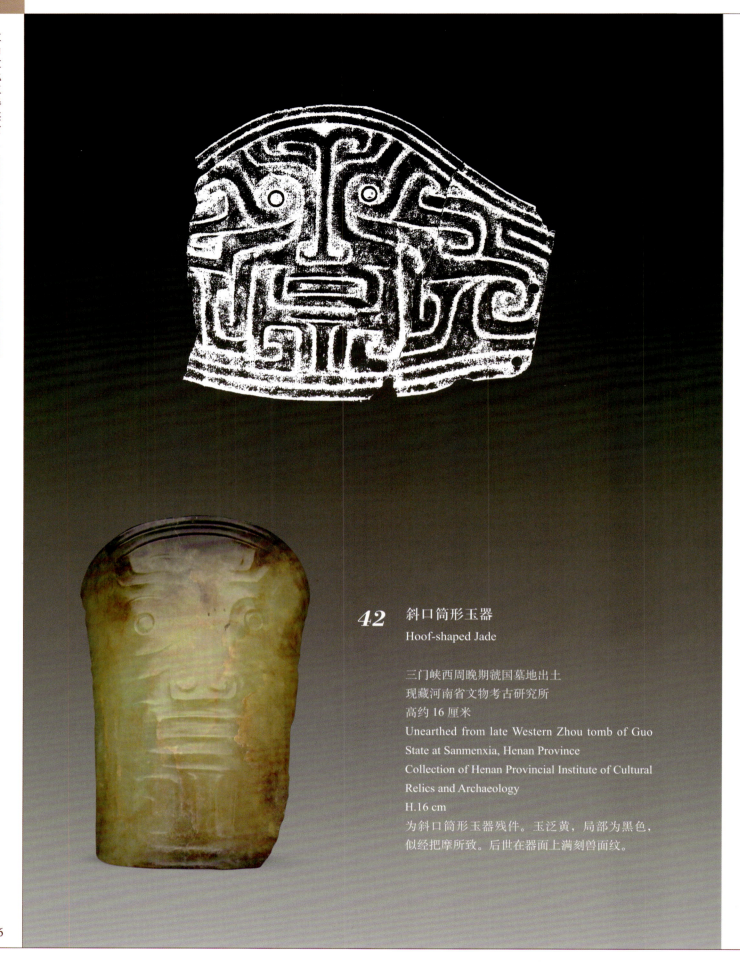

42 斜口筒形玉器
Hoof-shaped Jade

三门峡西周晚期虢国墓地出土
现藏河南省文物考古研究所
高约 16 厘米
Unearthed from late Western Zhou tomb of Guo
State at Sanmenxia, Henan Province
Collection of Henan Provincial Institute of Cultural
Relics and Archaeology
H.16 cm
为斜口筒形玉器残件。玉泛黄，局部为黑色，
似经把摩所致。后世在器面上满刻兽面纹。

44 玉雕龙

Jade Dragon

凤翔南指挥镇战国中期 3 号秦墓出土
现藏陕西省考古研究院
高 2.2、宽 1.8、厚 0.6 厘米
Unearthed from middle Warring States Tomb 3
of Qin State at Nanzhihui, Fengxiang
Collection of Shaanxi Provincial Institute of
Archaeology
H. 2.2 cm; W. 1.8 cm; T. 0.6 cm

发表于刘云辉主编：《中国出土玉器全集·14·陕西》(图版 25)，科学出版社，2005 年。
青玉，略泛白斑，呈首尾相连猪龙形象。器一面平整，另一面凸起，高浮雕一对上耸之大耳，两只耳朵内腔深浅不一，两耳头顶之间雕出凸起的狭长三角形。高额头，吻部前伸，有较长的阴线口缝，眼部为浅浮雕，中部略靠上对钻一圆孔，两面均呈马蹄形。该器虽出自战国秦墓之中，但玉器具有明显的红山文化风格。（刘云辉）

43 玉雕龙

Jade Dragon

43

44

2005 年韩城梁带村春秋晚期芮国墓地 26 号墓出土
现藏陕西省考古研究院
高 13.6、宽 11、厚 4.4、中心孔径 3、颈部孔径 1.1 厘米
Unearthed from Tomb 26 at late Spring and Autumn burial
ground of Rui State, Liangdai, Hancheng, 2005
Collection of Shaanxi Provincial Institute of Archaeology
H. 13.6 cm; W. 11 cm. T. 4.4 cm; Dia. (perforation)
(central) 3 cm, (neck) 1.1 cm

发表于《2005 中国重要考古发现》（第 81 页），文物出版社，2006 年。
发现时位于墓主人左肩上部。青绿岫岩玉质，大部分受沁呈褐红色，整体呈首尾相接的 "C" 形猪龙形象。猪龙头部硕大，圆弧状双耳竖起，双目圆睁，口微张，首尾相接处切割出 "V" 形缺口，器身中央对钻一圆孔，两面均呈马蹄形，颈部对钻一小圆孔，吻、鼻、额均琢出带 "V" 形沟槽的阴线纹。两面造型纹样基本相同。应是距今 5000 年前红山文化先人的遗物。（刘云辉）

45 勾云形玉器

Jade in the Shape of Hook and Cloud

2001 年凤翔上郭店春秋晚期墓出土
现藏凤翔县博物馆
长 11.4、宽 4.3、厚 0.15 ~ 0.3 厘米
Unearthed from late Spring and Autumn tomb at Shangguodian, Fengxiang, 2001
Collection of Fengxiang County Museum
L. 11.4 cm; W. 4.3 cm; T. 0.15 － 0.3 cm
发表于刘云辉主编：《中国出土玉器全集·14·陕西》(图版 26)，科学出版社，2005 年。

青玉质，呈青黄色，一侧中部有受沁白斑，片状，左右对称，整体为一带齿动物面形玉雕。玉器中央钻两个圆孔，为动物面之双睛，双圆睛周围为斜坡状，双目之上均镂出弧状透孔，中部上端平齐，居中钻一圆孔，左右两侧中部琢出长条状凸齿，凸齿中部均切割出条形孔，左右凸齿上部琢出互相对称的弧形，缺口朝下，双目之下琢出五组条形尖齿。动物面双目凸齿上下、弧形及五组齿上均琢磨出瓦沟形纹。两面造型和纹样相同。笔者认为它与常见的勾云形玉珮有别，表现的应是鸮锐利的双眼，弯而带钩的喙和爪及冠、翼、尾等，是玉鸮类猛禽的平面展出形式。（刘云辉）

2 有出土单位的收集品

COLLECTIONS UNEARTHED
FROM ARCHAEOLOGICAL POINTS

FUXIN, LIAONING PROVINCE

1. Jade in the Shape of Hook and Cloud
2. Jade Ring
3. Jade *Bi* Disc
4. Jade Sticks
5. Jade Bird
6. Jade Owl
7. Jade Owl
8. Jade Tortoise
9. Jade Tortoise

AOHAN, INNER MONGOLIA AUTONOMOUS REGION

10. Square Jade *Bi* Disc

辽宁阜新

1. 勾云形玉器

2. 玉环

3. 玉璧

4. 玉棒

5. 玉鸟

6. 玉鸮

7. 玉鸮

8. 玉龟

9. 玉龟

内蒙古敖汉旗

10. 方形玉璧

辽宁阜新
FUXIN, LIAONING PROVINCE

1 勾云形玉器（胡 M1：3）

Jade in the Shape of Hook and Cloud

阜新胡头沟红山文化墓葬出土
现藏辽宁省博物馆
残存长 7.9、宽 4.8、厚 0.6 厘米
Unearthed from Hongshan Culture tomb at Hutougou, Fuxin
Collection of Museum of Liaoning Province
L. (fragment) 7.9 cm; W. 4.8 cm; T. 0.6 cm
发表于《文物》1984 年 6 期，方殿春、刘葆华：《辽宁阜新县胡头沟红
山文化玉器墓的发现》（线图见第 3 页图七，3）。
乳白色，表面有腐蚀。边有残缺。中心透雕，呈卷云纹，四边出卷角，
器面磨出与纹饰相应走向的浅沟槽，上缘有双孔。

2 玉环（胡 M1 ： 2）

Jade Ring

阜新胡头沟红山文化墓葬出土

现藏辽宁省博物馆

直径 4.6、内径 3.5 厘米

Unearthed from Hongshan Culture tomb at Hutougou, Fuxin

Collection of Museum of Liaoning Province

Dia. 4.6 cm, (inner) 3.5 cm

发表于《文物》1984 年 6 期，方殿春、刘葆华：《辽宁阜新县胡

头沟红山文化玉器墓的发现》（线图见第 3 页图七，2）。

蛋白色，似蛇纹岩质。环边起棱，断面呈圆三角形，表面侵蚀较重，

且断为数段。

3 玉璧（胡 M1 ： 1）

Jade *Bi* Disc

阜新胡头沟红山文化墓葬出土
现藏辽宁省博物馆
直径 4、中心孔径 1.4、厚 0.2 厘米
Unearthed from Hongshan Culture tomb at Hutougou, Fuxin
Collection of Museum of Liaoning Province
Dia. 4 cm, (perforation) 1.4 cm; T. 0.2 cm
发表于《文物》1984 年 6 期，方殿春、刘葆华：《辽宁阜新县胡
头沟红山文化玉器墓的发现》（线图见第 3 页图七，1）。
青白色。体扁平，内外缘都为圆形，不够规则，近外边缘钻一小
圆孔，可能作系挂之用。

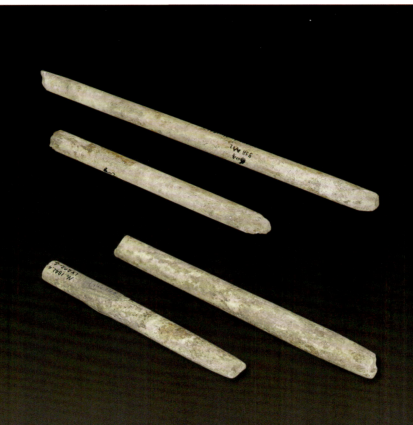

4 **玉棒**（胡 M1：10-1、胡 M1：10-2、胡 M1：10-3、胡 M1：10-4）
Jade Sticks

阜新胡头沟红山文化墓葬出土
现藏辽宁省文物考古研究所
胡 M1:10-1 长 30.9、直径 1.72 厘米
胡 M1:10-2 长 18.5、直径 1.72 厘米
胡 M1:10-3 长 19.3、直径 1.77 厘米
胡 M1:10-4 长 14.9、直径 1.64 厘米
Unearthed from Hongshan Culture tomb at Hutougou, Fuxin
Collection of Liaoning Provincial Institute of Cultural Relics and Archaeology
胡 M1:10-1 L. 30.9 cm; Dia. 1.72 cm
胡 M1:10-2 L. 18.5 cm; Dia. 1.72 cm
胡 M1:10-3 L. 19.3 cm; Dia. 1.77 cm
胡 M1:10-4 L. 14.9 cm; Dia. 1.64 cm
发表于《文物》1984 年 6 期，方殿春、刘葆华：《辽宁阜新县胡头沟红山文化玉器
墓的发现》（线图见第 3 页图七，10）。
四件可分两型：M1：10-1、M1：10-2 均一端磨出斜向平面；M1：10-3、
M1：10-4 的端部内收，从内收趋势看，约为尖状，而非磨出斜面。
牛河梁遗址第十六地点第 3 号墓也有玉棒形器随葬，形制近于胡头沟 1 号墓胡
M1：10-3、4，即棒头为尖状，且有明确出土位置，在人体左腰部，可供参照。
此类玉棒形器，虽形制单一，但长度可达二三十余厘米，可见所用玉料甚大，且
棒体直而正圆，加工应有难度。

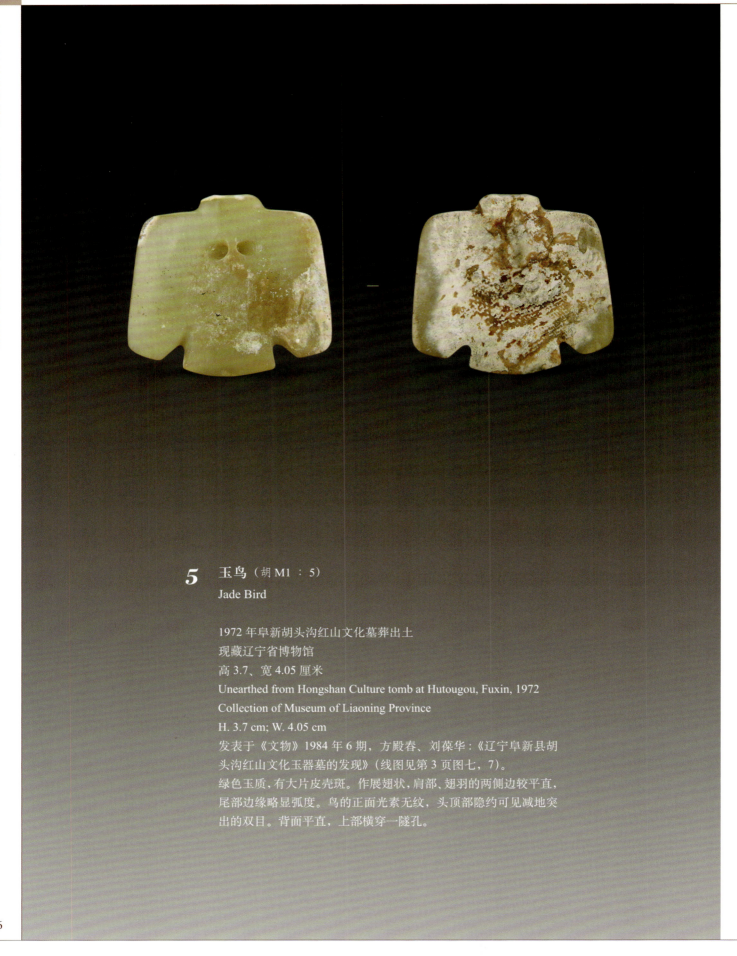

5 玉鸟（胡 M1：5）

Jade Bird

1972 年阜新胡头沟红山文化墓葬出土

现藏辽宁省博物馆

高 3.7、宽 4.05 厘米

Unearthed from Hongshan Culture tomb at Hutougou, Fuxin, 1972

Collection of Museum of Liaoning Province

H. 3.7 cm; W. 4.05 cm

发表于《文物》1984 年 6 期，方殿春、刘葆华：《辽宁阜新县胡头沟红山文化玉器墓的发现》（线图见第 3 页图七，7）。

绿色玉质，有大片皮壳斑。作展翅状，肩部、翅羽的两侧边较平直，尾部边缘略显弧度。鸟的正面光素无纹，头顶部隐约可见减地突出的双目。背面平直，上部横穿一隧孔。

6　玉鸮（胡 M1：9）

Jade Owl

1972 年阜新胡头沟红山文化墓葬出土
现藏辽宁省博物馆
长 3.1 厘米
Unearthed from Hongshan Culture tomb at Hutougou, Fuxin, 1972
Collection of Museum of Liaoning Province
L. 3.1 cm

发表于《文物》1984 年 6 期，方殿春、刘葆华：《辽宁阜新县胡头沟红山文化玉器墓的发现》（线图见第 3 页图七，9）。

淡绿色玉，有大片皮壳斑。正面展翅形，肩部、羽翅及尾部的边缘都作圆弧形。首部雕出双耳，也略显喙部，鸮翅较窄，短宽尾，以较宽的阴线雕出翅尾的羽纹。背面斜钻一隧孔。

7 玉鸮（胡M1∶8）

Jade Owl

阜新胡头沟红山文化墓葬出土
现藏辽宁省博物馆
长 2.5 厘米
Unearthed from Hongshan Culture tomb at Hutougou, Fuxin
Collection of Museum of Liaoning Province
L. 2.5 cm
发表于《文物》1984 年 6 期，方殿春、刘葆华：《辽宁阜新县胡头沟红山文化玉器墓的发现》（线图见第 3 页图七，8）。
淡绿色玉质，表面有大片皮壳。正面展翅形，肩部圆而耸，翅及尾部的外展都甚宽，显示出展翅飞翔的姿态。翅、尾有表现羽纹的刻线，尾部边缘的羽纹以波浪线表示。头部则以甚浅的圆雕表现耳和目。背面平，颈下横钻一隧孔。

8 玉龟（胡M1：7）

Jade Tortoise

阜新胡头沟红山文化墓葬出土
现藏辽宁省博物馆
长 4.8、宽 2.8、厚 0.5 厘米
Unearthed from Hongshan Culture tomb at Hutougou, Fuxin
Collection of Museum of Liaoning Province
L. 4.8 cm; W. 2.8 cm; T. 0.5 cm

发表于《文物》1984 年 6 期，方殿春、刘葆华：《辽宁阜新县胡
头沟红山文化玉器墓的发现》（线图见第 3 页图七，5）。

淡绿色玉质，泛黄色。通体光滑无纹。龟体较长，前部稍窄而后
部稍宽。龟颈前伸，头部近于三角形，吻前伸，以概略的棱线表
现口与目，尖尾较短，龟背部近于圆形，无其他细部表现，四足
收缩作爬行状。腹部以压地法将正中雕出一道直通首尾的突脊，
脊下有一横向对钻的穿孔，用以穿系，有如桥状纽。此龟通体无纹，
雕刻手法极为概略，却对龟的动态与神态有准确表现，是红山文
化玉器中一件精品。

玉龟还见于牛河梁遗址第五地点一号冢 1 号墓，为双龟，分别置
于左右手处，应为墓主人手握，是神权的生动表现，且为一雄一雌。
以上胡头沟 1 号墓所出两件玉龟，质地、造型差别均较大，是否
也为一对，存疑。

9 玉龟（胡M1：6）

Jade Tortoise

阜新胡头沟红山文化墓葬出土

现藏辽宁省博物馆

长 3.5、最宽处 3.6、厚 0.9 厘米

Unearthed from Hongshan Culture tomb at Hutougou, Fuxin

Collection of Museum of Liaoning Province

L. 3.5 cm; W. (max) 3.6 cm; T. 0.9 cm

发表于《文物》1984 年 6 期，方殿春、刘葆华：《辽宁阜新县胡头沟红山文化玉器墓的发现》（线图见第 3 页图七，6）。

青绿色，被大片黄白色瑕斑覆盖。整体作微缩形。龟首近于三角形，以短阴线雕出口与目。足蹼部也以多道短而宽的阴刻线表现。背微凸，近六角形，光素无纹。腹部颈下有一横钻的隧孔，用以穿系。

10　方形玉璧

Square Jade *Bi* Disc

敖汉旗草帽山积石冢石室墓出土
现藏敖汉旗博物馆
长 9.9、宽 9.4、内径 3.8~4.1、穿孔径 0.3~0.5、厚 0.3~0.5 厘米
Unearthed from stone tombs at Caomaoshan, Aohan
Collection of Aohan Banner Museum
L. 9.9 cm;W. 9.4 cm; Dia. (inner) 3.8 − 4.1 cm, (perforation) 0.3 − 0.5
cm; T. 0.3 − 0.5 cm
发表于《中国文物报》2001 年 9 月 26 日收藏鉴赏周刊 37 期,《红
山文化方形玉璧出土》。
白色,质较细腻。通体磨制,正方形,中间厚而四边薄,璧孔为单
面钻,近顶部边缘两面对钻一孔。
方形璧以前只见于山东龙山文化。现红山文化出土已不只一件,是
方形玉璧的最早实例,而以此件最为规范,且仍具有内外边缘薄的
红山文化玉璧特点。

3 遗址收集品

COLLECTIONS FROM ARCHAEOLOGICAL SITES

JIANPING AND LINGYUAN, LIAONING PROVINCE

1. Jade Dragon
2. Jade in the Shape of Hook and Cloud
3. Hoof-shaped Jade
4. Two-ring Jade *Bi* Disc

ONGNIUD, INNER MONGOLIA AUTONOMOUS REGION

5. Coiled Jade Dragon
6. Short Hook-shaped Jade
7. Hook-shaped Jade
8. Jade Ornamental Plaque

BAIRIN RIGHT BANNER, INNER MONGOLIA AUTONOMOUS REGION

9. Jade Dragon
10. Jade Dragon
11. Bird-shaped Jade *Jue* Ring
12. Jade Bird
13. Jade Bird
14. Jade Bird
15. Jade Silkworm Pupas
16. Jade Silkworm Pupa
17. Hook-shaped Jade
18. Jade in the Shape of Hook and Cloud
19. Three-ring Jade *Bi* Disc
20. Jade Beads

辽宁建平－凌源

1. 玉雕龙

2. 勾云形玉器

3. 斜口筒形玉器

4. 二联玉璧

内蒙古翁牛特旗

5. 附脊卷体玉雕龙

6. 短钩形玉器

7. 环钩形玉器

8. 玉牌饰

内蒙古巴林右旗

9. 玉雕龙

10. 玉雕龙

11. 鸟形玉玦

12. 玉鸟

13. 玉鸟

14. 玉鸟

15. 玉蚕蛹

16. 玉蚕蛹

17. 钩形玉器

18. 勾云形玉器

19. 三联璧形玉器

20. 玉串珠

辽宁建平—凌源

JIANPING AND LINGYUAN, LIAONING PROVINCE

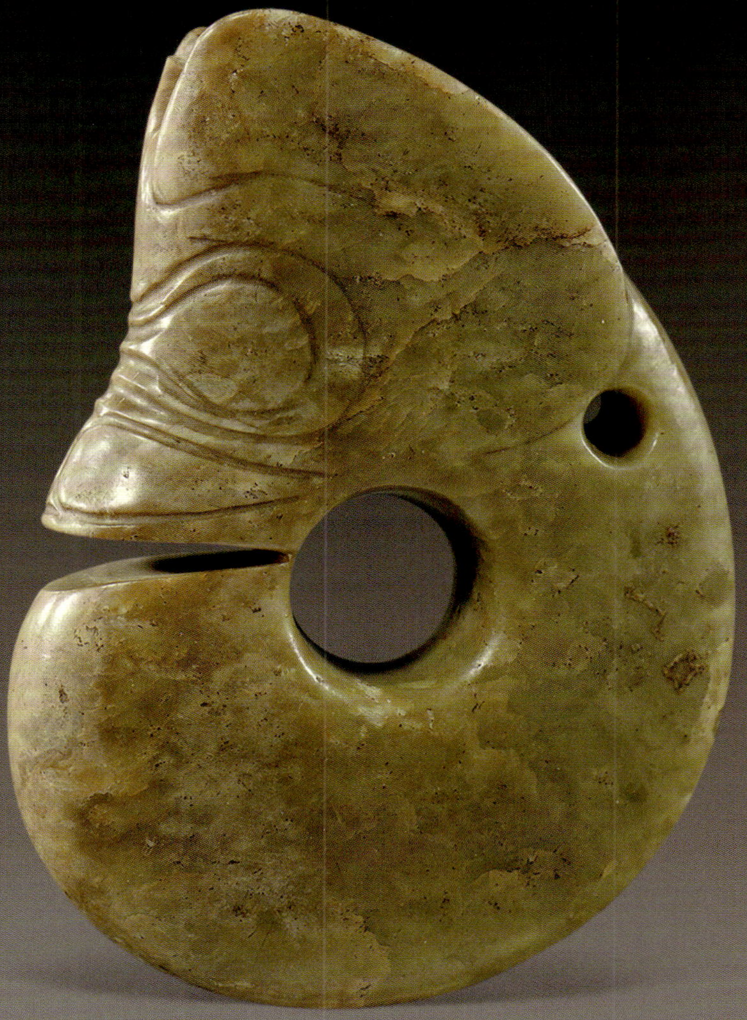

1 玉雕龙 (N 采：7)

Jade Dragon

1984 年于建平富山乡张福店征集

现藏辽宁省文物考古研究所

高 15、宽 10.2、厚 3.8 厘米

Acquired at Zhangfudian, Fushan, Jianping, 1984

Collection of Liaoning Provincial Institute of Cultural Relics and Archaeology

H. 15 cm; W. 10.2 cm; T. 3.8 cm

发表于辽宁省文物考古研究所编：《牛河梁红山文化遗址与玉器精粹》（第 53 页图 5），文物出版社，1997 年。

淡绿色，一面大部分为黄色皮壳，另一面耳部有裂纹，近底部有原玉料所遗凹坑点。环体，较扁平，缺口未切透，内缘相连，切口为平口，切面也经打磨光滑。大小孔都为两面对钻。以阴线刻出目、鼻，线条粗细不匀，以中部线条最为粗犷，由中部向两侧渐由粗到细，且线条较短，有多处接头，有的接头或错开，或相交，显草率。

2 勾云形玉器（N采：1）

Jade in the Shape of Hook and Cloud

20 世纪 40 年代收集

现藏辽宁省博物馆

长 22.4、宽 11.2、厚 0.8 厘米

Collected in the 1940s

Collection of Museum of Liaoning Province

L. 22.4 cm; W. 11.2 cm; T. 0.8 cm

发表于《文物》1984 年 6 期，孙守道、郭大顺：《论辽河流域的原始文明与龙的起源》（线图见第 15 页图四）。

一角卷钩残缺。尺寸与形状都接近于 N16M2：1（见本书 049）。淡绿色玉，间有淡红褐或黄白色瑕斑。体为长方板状，由中心及四角卷钩组成，体面有随卷钩磨出的浅瓦沟纹饰。有正、背面之分，背面无纹饰，也无缀孔。只中心卷钩部有一较粗的刻线。

20 世纪 40 年代，佟柱臣先生曾在凌源牛河梁梁下农家见到过这件缺了一角的勾云形玉器（见佟柱臣：《中国新石器时代文化的一些新迹象》，《中国东北地区和新石器时代考古论集》255 页，文物出版社，1989 年），可知这是第一件可以明确指认出土地点的红山文化玉器。

3 斜口筒形玉器 （N采：2）

Hoof-shaped Jade

1981 年于建平富山乡马家沟村村民马龙图处征集

现藏辽宁省文物考古研究所

长 16.4 厘米

Acquired at Majiagou, Fushan, Jianping, 1981

Collection of Liaoning Provincial Institute of Cultural Relics and Archaeology

L. 16.4 cm

发表于《文物》1984 年 6 期，孙守道、郭大顺：《论辽河流域的原始文明与龙的起源》（线图见第 14 页图六，1）。

深绿色，两侧有红褐色瑕斑，瑕斑处遗有原玉料岩面凹坑。一端大斜面，口端磨出内斜面，另端平口，略向内凹，端面磨成外斜面，平口近边两侧未见钻孔，却各有一缺口，内壁正中一小圆洞，一侧有上下直通的弧形凹槽，为用线切割掏芯时所遗痕迹。

1981 年 4 月考古工作者在辽宁省建平县马家沟村村民家见到这件玉器，并以探寻这件玉器的出土地为线索而发现了牛河梁遗址（第二地点），所以这是在红山文化考古史上起过重要作用的一件玉器。

4　二联玉璧（N 采：4）

Two-ring Jade *Bi* Disc

1981 年于建平富山乡马家沟村征集
现藏辽宁省博物馆
长 12.8、上宽 6.2、下宽 8 厘米
Acquired at Majiagou, Fushan, Jianping, 1981
Collection of Museum of Liaoning Province
L. 12.8 cm, W. (upper) 6.2 cm, (lower) 8 cm
发表于《文物》1984 年 6 期，孙守道、郭大顺：《论辽河
流域的原始文明与龙的起源》（线图见第 14 页图六，3）。
白色蛇纹岩质，边缘遗有原岩面凹坑点，通体磨光。璧体
较厚，边缘磨薄。上璧近于圆三角形，下璧近于正圆形，
两璧孔都为两面对钻。

5 附脊卷体玉雕龙
Coiled Jade Dragon

1971 年翁牛特旗赛沁塔拉（原称三星他拉）村
北出土
由翁牛特旗文化馆征集
现藏中国国家博物馆
高 26、脊饰长 21、厚 2.3~2.9、内孔径 0.3 厘米
Unearthed north of Saiqintala, Ongniud, 1971
Acquired by Ongniud Banner Cultural Centre
Collection of National Museum of China
H. 26 cm; L. (back ornament) 21 cm; T. 2.3 — 2.9
cm; Dia. (perforation) 0.3 cm

发表于《文物》1984 年 6 期，翁牛特旗文化馆：《内蒙古翁牛特旗三星他拉村发现玉龙》（线图见第 6 页图一）
及孙守道：《三星他拉红山文化玉龙考》。

长吻前伸，有脊饰（鬣）上卷，除头部外，通体光素无纹，体穿单孔。卷曲的身体与商代玉龙有近似
处，但制作技法与具体形象均与商代玉龙有很大不同。赛沁塔拉村在赤峰市以北百余公里，翁牛特旗
所在地乌丹镇西北约 10 公里处。村北有群山，山南为一片开阔地，玉龙的出土地点在山的南坡上，在
玉龙出土范围内只散布有红山文化的泥质红陶片和饰压印箆点"之"字纹陶片。从出土地点到山顶一带，
还分布有饰压印"之"字纹夹砂灰褐陶片，泥质红陶钵片，绘黑彩的彩陶片，石粗和石磨盘、石磨棒等。
而不见其他时代的遗存。

这件玉雕龙，用料大而质较纯，从整体到头部、附脊都甚为规整，是红山文化玉器中的精品。由于这
类附脊玉雕龙尚无正式出土的实例，目前有出土地点线索的两件，都在翁牛特旗境内，附近红山文化
遗址分布稀疏，却多见赵宝沟文化遗址，而赵宝沟文化的陶器上常有刻划的鹿形象，有据此推测这类
附脊玉雕龙，有属于赵宝沟文化的可能，附脊应为角的演变。又有以为这类附脊玉雕龙，为夏家店下
层文化遗物，由于夏家店下层文化遗址已发掘多处，玉器发现极少，大甸子墓葬虽有一些玉器随葬，
但多小件，夏商时期作风浓厚，又多为早期流传品，而翁牛特旗已是夏家店下层文化分布的北部边缘，
故此说不可信。

6　短钩形玉器

Short Hook-shaped Jade

翁牛特旗海日金山遗址出土

现藏翁牛特旗博物馆

长 2.6、宽 2.3、厚 0.25 厘米

Unearthed at Hairijinshan site, Ongniud

Collection of Ongniud Banner Museum

L. 2.6 cm; W. 2.3 cm; T. 0.25 cm

发表于《内蒙古文物考古》第 3 期，辽宁省博物馆文物工作队：《内蒙古翁牛特旗两处新石器时代遗址》（线图见第 17 页图十，3）

淡绿色，泛黄。体扁平，通体磨光。形如短角，上端宽，向下渐收形成卷钩。上端两边角各钻一小孔。此件形似勾云形玉器的一角，但又自成一器，是否为残器再加工，存疑。

7 环钩形玉器

Hook-shaped Jade

翁牛特旗海日金山遗址出土

现藏翁牛特旗博物馆

环径 6.2、厚 0.6 厘米

Unearthed at Hairijinshan site, Ongniud

Collection of Ongniud Banner Museum

Dia. 6.2 cm; T. 0.6 cm

发表于《内蒙古文物考古》第 3 期,辽宁省博物馆文物工作队:
《内蒙古翁牛特旗两处新石器时代遗址》(线图见第 17 页图十,7)
白色并布满淡青色斑纹。通体磨光。环体,横断面作椭圆形。
一端渐收如钩,两端都有残断,宽端有对钻的单孔。此器虽
十分简略,环体由宽到尖,变化匀称,制作甚精而费工,其
形有与玉雕龙近似处。

8 玉牌饰

Jade Ornamental Plaque

于翁牛特旗海日金山遗址采集
现藏翁牛特旗博物馆
长 4.3、宽 2.8、厚 0.4 厘米
Found at Hairijinshan site, Ongniud
Collection of Ongniud Banner Museum
L. 4.3 cm; W. 2.8 cm; T. 0.4 cm
发表于《内蒙古文物考古》第 3 期，辽宁省博物馆文物工作队：
《内蒙古翁牛特旗两处新石器时代遗址》(线图见第 17 页图十,4)
淡绿色，长方形。通体磨光，薄厚均匀，边侧磨出棱线。一端
近边缘处中间偏一侧对钻一小孔。此件造型甚为简洁，却十分
规整。在红山文化玉器中，这种长方形的造型还是唯一的实例。

9　玉雕龙

Jade Dragon

巴林右旗羊场乡额尔根勿苏遗址出土
现藏巴林右旗博物馆
高 16.6、宽 10.6、厚 2.9 厘米
Unearthed at Yangchang, Bairin Right Banner
Collection of Bairin Right Banner Museum
H. 16.6 cm; W. 10.6 cm; T. 2.9 cm
发表于《文物》1984 年 6 期，孙守道：《红山
文化玉龙考》（线图见第 9 页图六）。
青绿色，器表布满深色皮壳。形体大，头尾
相接处未切断。头部有圆弧形双立耳，较长，
吻部稍显突出，以阴刻线雕出圆目及唇鼻，
线条稀疏而显粗犷，鼻部并间以打洼。

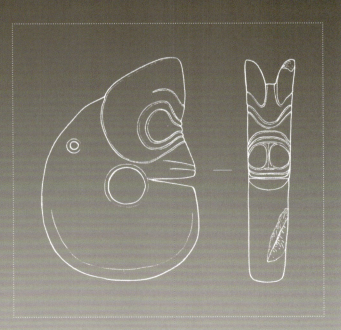

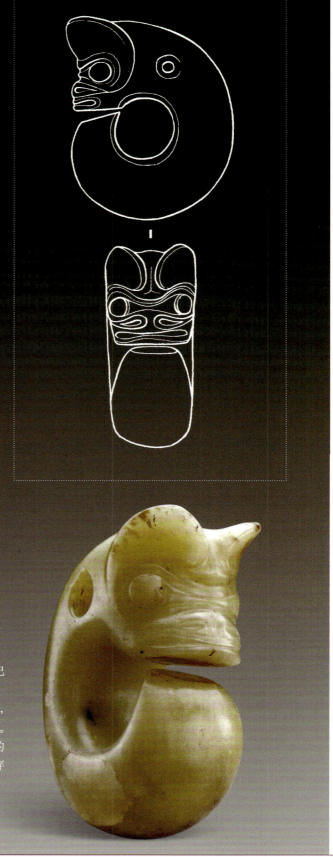

10 玉雕龙

Jade Dragon

巴林右旗巴彦汉苏木那日斯台遗址出土

20 世纪 80 年代初由巴林右旗博物馆征集

现藏巴林右旗博物馆

高 7.3、宽 5.1、中心孔径 2.8、厚 2.7 厘米

Unearthed at Bairin Right Banner

Acquired by Bairin Right Banner Museum in the early 1980s

Collection of Bairin Right Banner Museum

H. 7.3 cm; W. 5.1 cm; Dia. (perforation) 2.8 cm; T. 2.7 cm

发表于《考古》1987 年 6 期，巴林右旗博物馆：《内蒙巴林右旗那斯台遗址调查》（线图见第 517 页图一四，5）。

绿色，外侧有褐红色瑕斑和纹裂。体卷曲，横断面扁圆形，首尾相隔，额头与吻部隆起，面部显内凹，使头部形成三段。有圆弧状短耳，圆目突出，下颌前伸，以阴线刻出凸起的鼻与口。尾卷至末端尖，更显尾部内卷的有力。颈部对穿一圆孔，环体素面无纹。

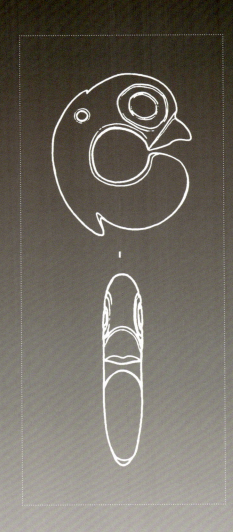

11 鸟形玉玦

Bird-shaped Jade *Jue* Ring

巴林右旗巴彦汉苏木那日斯台遗址出土
20世纪80年代初由巴林右旗博物馆征集
现藏巴林右旗博物馆
高5.5、宽4.9、厚1厘米
Unearthed at Bairin Right Banner
Acquired by Bairin Right Banner Museum in the early 1980s
Collection of Bairin Right Banner Museum
H. 5.5 cm; W. 4.9 cm; T. 1 cm

发表于《考古》1987年6期，巴林右旗博物馆：《内蒙巴林右旗那斯台遗址调查》（线图见第516页图一三，1）。

黄白色，应为蛇纹岩质。体卷曲，横断面为扁柱形，首尾相近。头与喙分界明显，喙似有残，端起尖。圆目，外围以阴刻的圆圈两周，使面部全为眼睛占据，形成巨目。卷体外侧边上下各起尖突，体上为短尖突，体下则起尖突甚为明显，如牙。尾端呈圆弧状，尾末端尖。颈后有钻孔，为两面对钻，孔较大。通体素面无纹，雕刻淳厚简朴。此件鸟形玦外边缘的下部起牙，上部颈后起短尖，头下与喙间也起尖如牙，与起三牙的牙璧有近似处，应非偶然。

12 玉鸟
Jade Bird

巴林右旗巴彦汉苏木那日斯台遗址出土
20 世纪 80 年代初由巴林右旗博物馆征集
现藏巴林右旗博物馆
高 2.5、宽 3、厚 0.8 厘米

Unearthed at Bairin Right Banner

Acquired by Bairin Right Banner Museum in the early
1980s

Collection of Bairin Right Banner Museum

H. 2.5 cm; W. 3 cm; T. 0.8 cm

发表于《考古》1987 年 6 期，巴林右旗博物馆：《内
蒙巴林右旗那斯台遗址调查》（线图见第 517 页图
一五，9）。

淡绿色，泛黄。形较小，溜肩，短翅，直尾。双目
圆鼓，脊背隆起，以较宽的压地和较粗的阳纹表现
翅羽。胸前有以三角形凹窝表现的鸟爪。背面靠近
头部有竖斜向隧孔，背面中部有横向桯钻痕，是选
用有钻孔遗留的玉料。

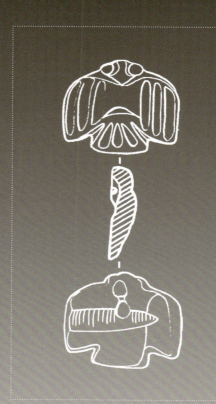

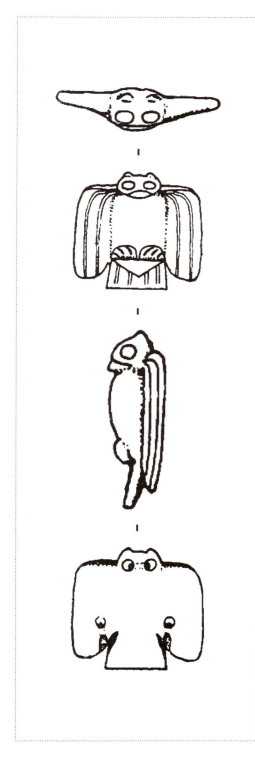

13 玉鸟

Jade Bird

巴林右旗巴彦汉苏木那日斯台遗址出土

20 世纪 80 年代初由巴林右旗博物馆征集

现藏巴林右旗博物馆

高 6.1、宽 6、厚 1.8 厘米

Unearthed at Bairin Right Banner

Acquired by Bairin Right Banner Museum in the early
1980s

Collection of Bairin Right Banner Museum

H. 6.1 cm; W. 6 cm; T. 1.8 cm

发表于《考古》1987 年 6 期，巴林右旗博物馆：《内
蒙巴林右旗那斯台遗址调查》（线图见第 517 页图
一四，8）。

淡绿色，泛黄，玉质莹泽细腻，光泽度高。双短耳耸立，
目浮雕，圆鼓较大，喙部短，喙端尖圆。双翅及尾平展，
平肩，翅翼稍有外斜，尾端直，翅与尾羽皆以阴刻
线表示，胸腹部鼓，下有以斜而短的阴线表现的双
爪，爪外凸明显，双爪附于尾面加饰的一三角形之上，
似作攀附状。鸟的背面平齐，上下部都有钻孔，近
头顶横钻一隧孔，下部翅尾交接处又各竖钻一隧孔。

14 玉鸟
Jade Bird

巴林右旗巴彦汉苏木那日斯台遗址出土
20 世纪 80 年代初由巴林右旗博物馆征集
现藏巴林右旗博物馆
高 4.4、宽 4.6、厚 1.7 厘米
Unearthed at Bairin Right Banner
Acquired by Bairin Right Banner Museum in the early 1980s
Collection of Bairin Right Banner Museum
H. 4.4 cm; W. 4.6 cm; T. 1.7 cm

发表于《考古》1987 年 6 期，巴林右旗博物馆：《内蒙巴林右旗那斯台遗址调查》(线图见第 517 页图一四，3)。
黄绿色，玉质纯，光泽度高。体近方形，头部近倒三角形。无耳，目圆鼓，目周围刻双阴线，三角形喙，长而宽，与胸部以甚深的刻槽相隔，使喙部外突尤显。肩与头端近平，由于翅羽线呈上斜走向，使肩部显上耸。翅末端显内收，尾端甚平。翅与尾面均用打洼技法形成阳纹式羽线，双翅的羽线在上部斜曲相连，尾羽短，中部打洼处较宽。胸腹部鼓，下置刻短阴线的双爪，双爪突出。鸟的背面平直，近顶部为横钻的三隧孔相通，并遗有为钻孔方便先作的斜竖短槽，中孔以下有一道竖立的桯钻痕，为选用先制器有钻孔遗留的玉料。

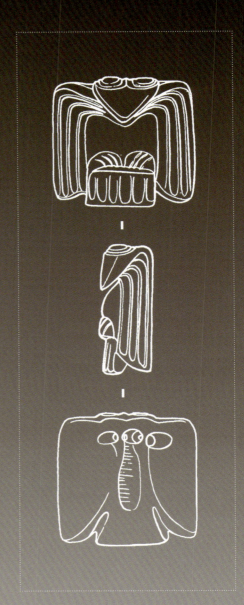

一

15 玉蚕蛹

Jade Silkworm Pupas

巴林右旗巴彦汉苏木那日斯台遗址出土
20 世纪 80 年代初由巴林右旗博物馆征集
现藏巴林右旗博物馆
长 7.3、宽 3.1、厚 2.6 厘米
Unearthed at Bairin Right Banner
Acquired by Bairin Right Banner Museum in the early 1980s
Collection of Bairin Right Banner Museum
L. 7.3 cm; W. 3.1 cm; T. 2.6 cm

发表于《考古》1987 年 6 期，巴林右旗博物馆：《内蒙巴
林右旗那斯台遗址调查》（线图见第 517 页图一四. 6）；
郭大顺：《红山文化有玉蚕吗？》，（台）《故宫文物月刊》
266 号，第二十三卷第二期，2005 年。

2 件，形制相同，黄绿色，两端有红褐色瑕斑。圆柱体。
前端较粗。头部有椭圆形的平端面，端面上边缘起甚短的
双乳突，是为触角，双目在端面中部偏下，围以两周阴刻线，
双目间起一竖行凸线与口相连，口作微张吐物状。蚕体有
下弯趋势，下腹部饰减地阳纹，其中前部以对向回字纹表
现双翼，后部以两道平行线表示腹节。体近前由两侧对钻
一孔，用以表现蚕的排孔。这类玉蚕蛹在红山文化玉器中
出现已有一定数量，但仍以此两件形态最为明确。初发表
时，误倒置，更有以为其形象为蝉，不确。（上图为倒置）

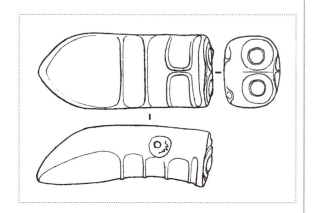

16 玉蚕蛹

Jade Silkworm Pupa

巴林右旗巴彦汉苏木那日斯台遗址出土
20 世纪 80 年代初由巴林右旗博物馆征集
现藏巴林右旗博物馆
长 9.3、直径 3.8 厘米
Unearthed at Bairin Right Banner
Acquired by Bairin Right Banner Museum in the early
1980s
Collection of Bairin Right Banner Museum
L. 9.3 cm; Dia. 3.8 cm

发表于《考古》1987 年 6 期，巴林右旗博物馆：《内蒙巴林右旗那斯台遗址调查》（线图见第 517 页图一四，7）。

黄绿色。形近前例，只个体稍大。双乳突状触角甚短，双目在头部端面中部，下以倒"八"字形阴刻纹表现口部，蚕体前平，近尾部下弯，下腹部以减地阳纹雕出四道阳纹，表示腹节。也在体近前两侧对钻一表现蚕排孔的单孔。与前例最大的不同是由头端双目间钻一孔直透尾端，在体中与侧孔相交。同形还有一件。（上两图为倒置）

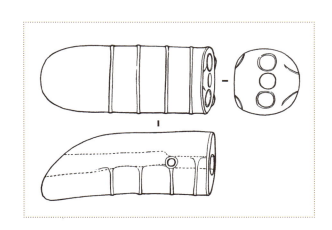

17 钩形玉器

Hook-shaped Jade

巴林右旗巴彦汉苏木那日斯台遗址出土
20 世纪 80 年代初由巴林右旗博物馆征集
现藏巴林右旗博物馆
长 6.8、宽 2.4、厚 0.8 厘米
Unearthed at Bairin Right Banner
Acquired by Bairin Right Banner Museum in the early 1980s
Collection of Bairin Right Banner Museum
L. 6.8 cm; W. 2.4 cm; T. 0.8 cm

发表于《考古》1987 年 6 期，巴林右旗博物馆：《内蒙巴林右旗那斯台遗址调查》（线图见第 516 页图一三，7）。

绿色。扁平条状，可分为钩体、栏和柄三部分。钩体形状和中部瓦沟纹都酷似勾云形玉器的一角，栏部为平行双凸棱，棱间刻槽较深。柄部较短，柄端从两侧磨薄为榫，榫与柄之间分界明显，榫面近端处对钻一单孔。可知此类器应为一种复合器。另，体面下部遗有一竖行的桯钻痕，且钻痕从柄端与榫的分界直至栏部双棱，为选用同一块玉料的其他器类桯钻孔壁的遗留，也是当时节省玉料的表现。

18　勾云形玉器

Jade in the Shape of Hook and Cloud

巴林右旗巴彦汉苏木那日斯台遗址出土
20 世纪 80 年代初由巴林右旗博物馆征集
现藏巴林右旗博物馆
长 18.1、宽 10.8、厚 0.7 厘米
Unearthed at Bairin Right Banner
Acquired by Bairin Right Banner Museum in the early 1980s
Collection of Bairin Right Banner Museum
L. 18.1 cm; W. 10.8 cm; T. 0.7 cm
发表于《考古》1987 年 6 期，巴林右旗博物馆：《内蒙巴林右旗
那斯台遗址调查》（线图见第 516 页图一三，7）。
黄白色，淡黄中少许泛绿，玉质中杂长石辉闪晶点。板状体，整
体和四角卷钩都较为平直，正面有随卷钩的浅槽线，不显打洼，
也缺少瓦沟纹的效果。背面平，近顶部有对穿的双孔。
此件勾云形玉器所用黄白色杂长石辉闪晶点的玉料及较为呆板的
形制和缺少打洼的纹饰，都与红山文化所常见的勾云形玉器有所
不同，是否反映区域特点，有待进一步的发现和研究。

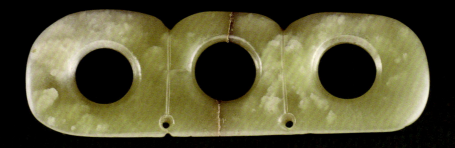

19 **三联璧形玉器**

Three-ring Jade *Bi* Disc

巴林右旗巴彦汉苏木那日斯台遗址出土
20 世纪 80 年代初由巴林右旗博物馆征集
现藏巴林右旗博物馆
长 11.9、宽 3.9、厚 0.6、孔径为 1.7~1.6 厘米
Unearthed at Bairin Right Banner
Acquired by Bairin Right Banner Museum in the early 1980s
Collection of Bairin Right Banner Museum
L. 11.9 cm; W. 3.9 cm; T. 0.6 cm; Dia. (perforation) 1.7 – 1.6 cm
发表于《考古》1987 年 6 期，巴林右旗博物馆：《内蒙巴林右旗那斯
台遗址调查》（线图见第 517 页图一四，2）。
绿色。为三璧相连成长条形，各个璧都具有外缘方圆、内缘近于正圆、
边薄似刃的特点。长边的一侧为三联弧形，长边的另一侧平齐，近边
并钻对称双小孔。三璧之间各以竖长横短的十字形阴刻线相隔。
此三联璧形器长边一侧起三弧另一侧平的造型，不同于红山文化常见
的三联璧，而接近于红山文化另一种有为梳背饰的三孔形器，如是，
则应以平边为底的横置为正常置法。

20 **玉串珠**

Jade Beads (68)

巴林右旗巴彦汉苏木那日斯台遗址出土

20 世纪 80 年代初由巴林右旗博物馆征集

现藏巴林右旗博物馆

直径 1.3~2.3 厘米

Unearthed at Bairin Right Banner

Acquired at Bairin Right Banner Museum in the early 1980s

 Collection of BairinRight Banner Museum

Dia. 1.3-2.3 cm

发表于《考古》1987 年 6 期，巴林右旗博物馆：《内蒙巴林右旗那斯
台遗址调查》（线图见第 517 页图一五．3、4）。

68 颗，器形近于正圆形，体扁，正面圆鼓，背面平，并对钻一隧孔。

4 有出土地点的收集品
COLLECTIONS UNEARTHED FROM CERTAIN SITES

FUXIN,LIAONING PROVINCE

1. Jade Bird

2. Jade Axe

3. Jade Pendant in the Shape of Hook and Cloud

BAIRIN LEFT BANNER, INNER MONGOLIA AUTONOMOUS REGION

4. Jade Dragon

5. Hoof-shaped Jade

BAIRIN RIGHT BANNER, INNER MONGOLIA AUTONOMOUS REGION

6. Hoof-shaped Jade

7. Hoof-shaped Jade

8. Jade in the Shape of Hook and Cloud

9. Jade in the Shape of Hook and Cloud

ONGNIUD, INNER MONGOLIA AUTONOMOUS REGION

10. Coiled Jade Dragon

11. Jade *Yue* Battle-axe

12. Jade Axe

AOHAN, INNER MONGOLIA AUTONOMOUS REGION

13. Jade Dragon

14. Jade Dragon

15. Jade Dragon

16. Inner Part from Hoof-shaped Jade

17. Semifinished Hoof-shaped Jade

18. Hoof-shaped Jade

HEXIGTEN, INNER MONGOLIA AUTONOMOUS REGION

19. Hoof-shaped Jade

TONGLIAO, INNER MONGOLIA AUTONOMOUS REGION

20. Jade in the Shape of Hook and Cloud

HE BEI PROVINCE

21. Jade Dragon

辽宁阜新

1. 玉鸟

2. 玉斧

3. 勾云形玉器

内蒙古巴林左旗

4. 玉雕龙

5. 斜口筒形玉器

内蒙古巴林右旗

6. 斜口筒形玉器

7. 斜口筒形玉器

8. 勾云形玉器

9. 勾云形玉器

内蒙古翁牛特旗

10. 附脊玉雕龙

11. 玉钺

12. 玉斧

内蒙古敖汉旗

13. 玉雕龙

14. 玉雕龙

15. 玉雕龙

16. 斜口筒形玉器芯料

17. 斜口筒形玉器坯料

18. 斜口筒形玉器

内蒙古克什克腾旗

19. 斜口筒形玉器

内蒙古通辽

20. 勾云形玉器

河北

21. 玉雕龙

辽宁阜新
FUXIN, LIAONING PROVINCE

2 玉斧
Jade Axe

于阜新他本扎兰乡白玉都村收集
现藏阜新市博物馆
长 22.6、宽 9.6、厚 1.3 厘米
Collected at Baiyudu, Tabenzhalan, Fuxin
Collection of Fuxin Museum
L. 22.6 cm; W. 9.6 cm; T. 1.3 cm
色淡绿偏黄，通体磨制，较为光泽。器身甚
为扁平，如铲，中间略厚，器身两侧显外弧，
刃部呈圆弧状，顶部也作呈圆弧形，且顶端
也薄如刃。（胡健）

1

1 玉鸟
Jade Bird

阜新福兴地乡出土
现藏辽宁省博物馆
高 3.1、宽 3.6 厘米
Unearthed at Fuxingdi, Fuxin
Collection of Museum of Liaoning Province
H. 3.1 cm; W. 3.6 cm
发表于《文物》1984 年 6 期，孙守道、郭大顺：《论
辽河流域的原始文明与龙的起源》（线图见第
13 页图三，1）。
淡青色，透绿。雕线简略分明，头及胸部厚，
以下渐薄。双目以阴刻线雕在顶面，喙部三
角形，喙端圆尖状，平肩，翅下端圆，尾端
以波浪纹表现尾羽。腹部一突起的横宽带，
以下的尾面刻阴线三角状纹。背面平直，上
部横钻一隧孔。

2

3 勾云形玉器

Jade Pendant in the Shape of Hook and Cloud

1999 年于阜新紫都台乡毛德营子村收集

现藏阜新市博物馆

长 6.5、宽 2.5、厚 0.2 厘米

Collected at Maodeyingzi, Zidutai, Fuxin, 1999

Collection of Fuxin Museum

L. 6.5 cm; W. 2.5 cm; T .0.2 cm

乳白色，通体磨光，体形甚小。勾云形，长侧一端
为圆弧顶，近边缘对钻三孔，近顶部并刻一道横向
隐槽。长侧另端呈三突齿状。（胡健）

内蒙古巴林左旗
BAIRIN LEFT BANNER, INNER MONGOLIA AUTONOMOUS REGION

4 玉雕龙

Jade Dragon

1976 年于巴林左旗十三敖巴乡尖山子村刘家屯东山西坡采集

1986 年由巴林左旗博物馆征集

现藏巴林左旗博物馆

高 8.2、宽 6.2、厚 3.4 厘米

Found at Liujiatun, Bairin Left Banner, 1976

Acquired by Bairin Left Banner Museum, 1986

Collection of Bairin Left Banner Museum

H. 8.2 cm; W. 6.2 cm; T. 3.4 cm

发表于《辽海文物学刊》1994 年 1 期，王未想：《巴林左旗出土的红山文化玉器》（线图见第 15 页图三）。

鸡骨白玉。有黑色纹理和斑点。此件与常见玉雕龙相比，体态和雕工都有所不同。头部刻纹较为粗犷。内孔缘中部遗有两面对钻所留高脊。系孔较大。体较细，首尾间缺口较宽。双耳宽厚而较圆，目略呈扁圆状，有长鼻孔的表现。背有刻划符号，为阴文。

5　斜口筒形玉器

Hoof-shaped Jade

1964 年于巴林左旗杨家营子镇葛家营子村东北山坡采集

1977 年由巴林左旗博物馆征集

现藏巴林左旗博物馆

高 13、口径 6.5~8.2、底径 6.0~7.2 厘米

Found at Gejiayingzi, Bairin Left Banner, 1964

Acquired by Bairin Left Banner Museum, 1977

Collection of Bairin Left Banner Museum

H. 13 cm; Dia. (top) 6.5 — 8.2 cm, (bottom) 6 — 7.2 cm

发表于《辽海文物学刊》1994 年 1 期，王未想：《巴林左旗出土的红山文化玉器》（线图见第 15 页图二）

黄绿色，有红褐斑。椭圆形筒状，一端大，呈斜坡状口，一端小，为平口，边缘磨薄似刃，筒内壁制作痕迹明显。无钻孔。

6 斜口筒形玉器
Hoof-shaped Jade

1982 年于巴林右旗查干木伦苏木征集
现藏巴林右旗博物馆
高 7.6~12.5、直径 6.77~7.63、壁厚 0.62 厘米
Acquired at Bairin Right Banner, 1982
Collection of Bairin Right Banner Museum
H. 7.6 – 12.5 cm; Dia. 6.77 – 7.63 cm; T. 0.62 cm
发表于于建设主编:《红山玉器》(第 160 页),远方出版社,2004 年。
淡绿色,泛黄。有褐红色瑕斑和裂纹。长边一侧稍显内凹。平口
与斜口的边缘均磨薄似刃。平口两端均无钻孔。

7 斜口筒形玉器

Hoof-shaped Jade

1979 年于巴林右旗巴彦查干苏木征集

现藏巴林右旗博物馆

通长 11.5~19、直径 7.62~8.67、孔径 6.49~8.36、壁厚 0.6~0.75 厘米

Acquired at Bairin Right Banner, 1979

Collection of Bairin Right Banner Museum

L. 11.5 − 19 cm; Dia. 7.62 − 8.67 cm, (perforation) 6.49 − 8.36 cm; T. 0.6 − 0.75 cm

发表于于建设主编:《红山玉器》(第 158 页),远方出版社,2004 年。

墨绿色。器体较长,侧壁较直。平口与斜口边缘均磨薄似刃,平口端无钻孔。

8　勾云形玉器

Jade in the Shape of Hook and Cloud

巴林右旗巴彦塔拉苏木苏达勒嘎查出土
现藏巴林右旗博物馆
长 11.8、宽 12.5、厚 0.8 厘米
Unearthed at Bairin Right Banner
Collection of Bairin Right Banner Museum
L. 12.5 cm; W. 11.8 cm; T. 0.8 cm
发表于杨伯达主编：《中国玉文化玉学论丛 三编上》，乌兰：《巴林右旗
出土的红山诸文化玉器种类与纹饰》（彩图一），紫禁城出版社，2005 年。
深绿色，有瑕斑。为单钩形。整体近于方形。造型除具一般单钩形勾云
形玉器共同特征即中心与四角卷勾、随体形变化在面上磨出瓦沟纹以外，
在两侧上部有长体垂饰，垂饰上下起突棱，并饰弦纹。尤其值得注意的是，
中心卷钩下的一侧起对称双齿突，这种齿突为双钩形勾云形玉器所必备，
在单钩形勾云形玉器中极少见，可证单钩形与双钩形为同类器，即都属
于勾云形玉器，也证明双钩形勾云形玉器的齿突非人或兽的牙齿，双钩
形勾云形玉器也非人或兽面，而是单钩形勾云形玉器的结合体。

9 勾云形玉器

Jade in the Shape of Hook and Cloud

巴林右旗查干诺尔苏木出土
现藏巴林右旗博物馆
长 12.2、宽 4、厚 0.4 厘米
Unearthed at Bairin Right Banner
Collection of Bairin Right Banner Museum
L. 12.2 cm; W. 4 cm; T. 0.4 cm
发表于杨伯达主编：《中国玉文化玉学论丛 三编上》，乌兰：《巴林右旗
出土的红山诸文化玉器种类与纹饰》（彩图二），紫禁城出版社，2005 年。
白色，近于鸡骨白。为双钩形勾云形玉器。长边近边处中部钻一小孔，
此长边一侧有残缺，残缺旁另钻两小孔。此器体形较小而薄，但体面所
雕瓦沟纹较深，从而各部位如卷钩、齿突等都甚为显露。短边两侧中部
向外突出部分较长。

内蒙古翁牛特旗
ONGNIUD, INNER MONGOLIA AUTONOMOUS REGION

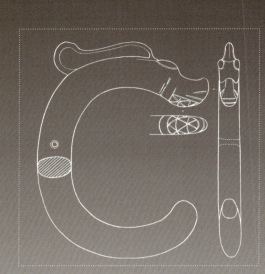

10　附脊玉雕龙

Coiled Jade Dragon

传翁牛特旗广德公乡黄谷屯出土
现藏翁牛特旗博物馆
高 16.7、身宽 2.6、鬣长 7.2、厚 1.8 厘米
Reportedly unearthed at Huanggutun, Ongniud
Collection of Ongniud Banner Museum
H. 16.7 cm; W. (body) 2.6 cm; L. (mane) 7.2 cm; T. 1.8 cm
发表于《中国文物报》1988 年 4 月 8 日一版，《内蒙古
又发现一件新石器时代玉龙》。
黄色，微泛淡绿，吻及尾端显褚红色石皮。形同赛沁塔
拉龙而体形较小，吻端不是平面，而为圆形且有上翘，
端面饰刻划短线而无表现鼻孔的双小洞，额底有网格刻
线纹，但较疏朗，鬣较短，鬣面打洼，端不起尖而呈圆端，
十分接近于勾云形玉器的一角。龙背钻孔在近于中部处，
鬣外一侧孔缘有明显磨痕，可证为系以悬挂之用。

11　玉钺

Jade *Yue* Battle-axe

翁牛特旗山嘴子乡大新井出土
现藏翁牛特旗博物馆
长 22、宽 17.1、厚 1.4 厘米
Unearthed at Daxinjing, Ongniud
Collection of Ongniud Banner Museum
L. 22 cm; W. 17.1 cm; T. 1.4 cm
发表于于建设主编:《红山玉器》(第 87 页),远方出版社,2004 年。
墨玉。侧边有残缺,刃部完整。形体较大,体较扁长而薄。顶
及两侧边均稍有外弧,刃部圆弧形。

12 玉斧
Jade Axe

翁牛特旗广德公乡小洼子村出土
现藏翁牛特旗博物馆
长 13.2、宽 5.2、厚 2.3 厘米
Unearthed at Xiaowazi, Ongniud
Collection of Ongniud Banner Museum
L. 13.2 cm; W. 5.2 cm; T. 2.3 cm
发表于于建设主编：《红山玉器》（第 82 页），远方出版
社，2004 年。
绿色。通体磨制，一侧边有片切割痕。体较长、顶及刃
圆弧形，刃边向一侧倾斜，两侧边也稍显外弧，体中较厚，
横断面呈椭圆形。

13 玉雕龙

Jade Dragon

敖汉旗萨力巴乡干饭营子出土
现藏敖汉旗博物馆
高 7.5、宽 6.3、厚 2.4 厘米
Unearthed at Ganfanyingzi, Aohan
Collection of Aohan Banner Museum
H. 7.5 cm; W. 6.3 cm; T. 2.4 cm
发表于邵国田主编：《敖汉文物精华》（第 67 页），内蒙
古文化出版社，2004 年。
墨绿色。耳有残缺。环体，体的两侧面较平。圆睛外突，
有鼻孔，嘴似张开状。此件以阴线与起地阳纹相结合的
雕刻技法，将面部五官的层次表现得甚为显露，不仅圆
睛突起，吻部鼻、嘴区分明显，尤其是雕出甚圆的鼻孔，
为所见同类玉雕龙中唯一一例。

14 玉雕龙

Jade Dragon

敖汉旗下洼镇河西出土

现藏敖汉旗博物馆

高 7.1、宽 5.9、中孔径 1.6~1.9、小孔径 0.2~0.6、体厚 2.1 厘米

Unearthed at Xiawa, Aohan

Collection of Aohan Banner Museum

H. 7.1 cm; W. 5.9 cm; Dia. (perforation) (middle) 1.6 — 1.9 cm, (small) 0.2 — 0.6 cm; T. 2.1 cm

发表于《文物》1984 年 6 期，孙守道、郭大顺：《论辽河流域的原始文明与龙的起源》（线图见第 13 页图三，4）。

淡绿色玉，玉质较纯，有红褐色瑕斑及裂纹。体较小，约为大型同类器的一半。头尾断开，断开后未过多琢磨，至使头尾端都有明显的起尖。圆目中雕出菱形突睛，双鼻孔较显。系孔不在中部，而在十分靠近头部的耳下。

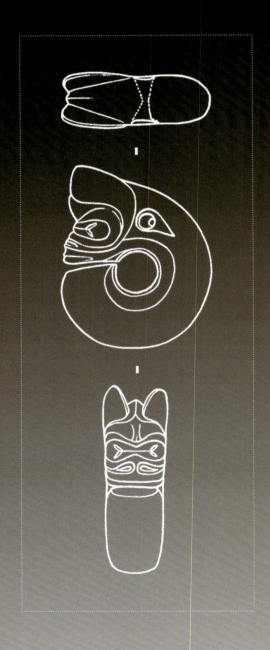

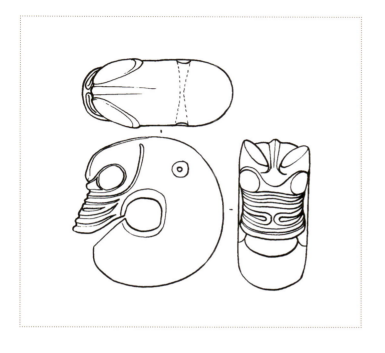

15　玉雕龙

Jade Dragon

敖汉旗牛古吐乡大五家出土
现藏敖汉旗博物馆
高 5.1、宽 5、大孔径 1.3、小孔径 0.5 厘米
Unearthed at Dawujia, Aohan
Collection of Aohan Banner Museum
H. 5.1 cm; W. 5 cm; Dia. (perforation) (big) 1.3
cm, (small) 0.5 cm
发表于邵国田主编:《敖汉文物精华》(第 67 页),
内蒙古文化出版社,2004 年。
淡绿色,有白色斑点。体较小而头部较长,吻
部尤长且前伸。耳则甚短而宽,头顶起脊明显
且延伸至背部,为此类玉雕龙中造型较有个性
的一件。

16

17　斜口筒形玉器坯料
Semifinished Hoof-shaped Jade

敖汉旗大甸子乡大瓜翘出土
现藏敖汉旗博物馆
高 16.7、大径 12、小径 7 厘米
Unearthed at Daguachi, Aohan
Collection of Aohan Banner Museum
H. 16.7 cm; Dia. (long) 12 cm, (short) 7 cm
发表于邵国田主编：《敖汉文物精华》（第 67 页），
内蒙古文化出版社，2004 年。

碧绿色，有大片白色斑痕。通体琢磨，间有打制痕。
椭圆形扁体，一端平，另端斜，近于斜口筒形玉器
外形。斜面一端有打击后的切割痕，为两道略弧的
切线，平面一端为磨平后又打制出一横行凹槽。应
为一斜口筒形玉器半成品，可观察到斜口筒形玉器
制作过程和工艺，是一件对研究红山文化玉器的制
作有重要价值的标本。

16　斜口筒形玉器芯料
Inner Part from Hoof-shaped Jade

敖汉旗骆驼营子小东山出土
现藏敖汉旗博物馆
高 11.2、大径 6.2、厚 3.3 厘米
Unearthed at Xiaodongshan, Aohan
Collection of Aohan Banner Museum
H. 11.2 cm; Dia. (long) 6.2 cm; T. 3.3 cm
发表于邵国田主编：《敖汉文物精华》（第 67 页），
内蒙古文化出版社，2004 年。

深绿色。通体磨光。两侧内弧，体形呈亚腰形。一端
较宽，一端较窄，有纵向凹槽由较窄一端直通体中，
凹槽由宽而窄而尖，尖端以上并有两圆窝，凹槽旁显
线切割痕迹。疑为制作斜口筒形玉器时掏出的内芯，
是又一件研究红山文化玉器制作工艺的重要标本。

17

18　斜口筒形玉器

Hoof-shaped Jade

敖汉旗烧锅地村出土
现藏敖汉旗博物馆
高 15.3、孔径 9.4 厘米
Unearthed at Shaoguodi, Aohan
Collection of Aohan Banner Museum
H. 15.3 cm; Dia. (perforation) 9.4 cm
发表于邵国田主编：《敖汉文物精华》（第 69 页），
内蒙古文化出版社，2004 年。
淡绿色，泛黄。有裂纹及褐色瑕斑。通体磨光，
内壁遗有纵向线弧形切线痕。无钻孔。

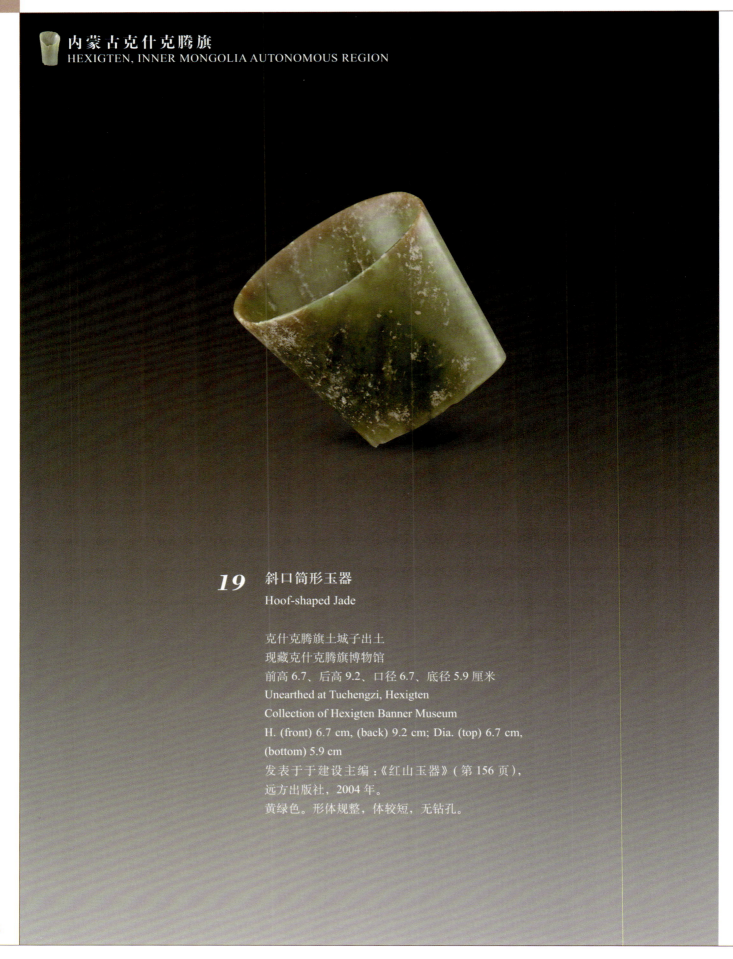

19　斜口筒形玉器

Hoof-shaped Jade

克什克腾旗土城子出土
现藏克什克腾旗博物馆
前高 6.7、后高 9.2、口径 6.7、底径 5.9 厘米
Unearthed at Tuchengzi, Hexigten
Collection of Hexigten Banner Museum
H. (front) 6.7 cm, (back) 9.2 cm; Dia. (top) 6.7 cm,
(bottom) 5.9 cm
发表于于建设主编:《红山玉器》(第 156 页),
远方出版社,2004 年。
黄绿色。形体规整,体较短,无钻孔。

20　勾云形玉器

Jade in the Shape of Hook and Cloud

于通辽科尔沁左翼中旗胜利乡塔拉村征集

现藏通辽市博物馆

长 15.6、宽 6.0、厚 0.3 厘米

Acquired at Tala, Horqin Left Wing Middle Banner, Tongliao

Collection of Tongliao Museum

L. 15.6 cm; W. 6 cm; T. 0.3 cm

发表于《中国文物报》1998 年 8 月 23 日第四版。

深绿色，一角有褐色瑕斑。双钩形，器体较厚。长边一侧正中钻一单孔，孔较大。长边另一侧有五组齿突。器面以较深而窄的打注形成随器形走向的瓦沟纹。此器缺左下角。

按：这类勾云形玉器特别是双钩形勾云形玉器，常以残缺形出现。牛河梁遗址还发现有以残钩随葬的情况。

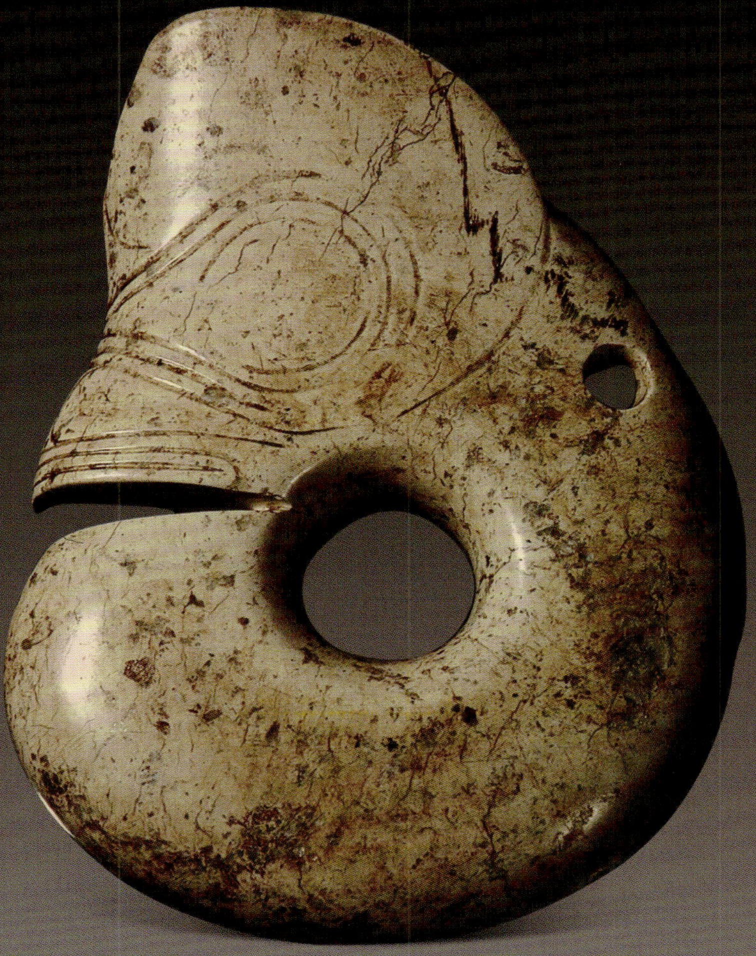

玉雕龙
Jade Dragon

河北围场下伙房收集
原藏围场县博物馆
高 14、最宽 10、最厚 3 厘米
Collected at Xiahuofang, Weichang, Hebei Province
Fromer Weichang County Museum
H. 14 cm; W. (max) 10 cm; T. (max) 3 cm
发表于《中国玉器全集·1·原始社会》（图版
二八），河北美术出版社，1992 年。
首肥大，双耳耸立，由三圈阴线勾画出圆形大眼，
首尾衔接处缺而不断，背有一穿。

5 有出土地区的收集品

COLLECTIONS UNEARTHED FROM CERTAIN REGIONS

FUXIN, LIAONING PROVINCE

1. Jade in the Shape of *Zhang* Tablet
2. Jade Bracelet
3. Jade in the Shape of *Gui* Tablet

JIANPING, LIAONING PROVINCE

4. Jade Dragon

CHAOYANG, LIAONING PROVINCE

5. Jade Silkworm Pupa
6. Jade *Bi* Disc
7. Jade Axe
8. Jade in the Shape of Hook and Cloud

AOHAN, INNER MONGOLIA AUTONOMOUS REGION

9. Jade in the Shape of Hook and Cloud
10. Jade Owl

CHIFENG, INNER MONGOLIA AUTONOMOUS REGION

11. Jade in the Shape of Hook and Cloud

辽宁阜新

1. "璋"形玉器

2. 玉镯

3. 圭形玉器

辽宁建平

4. 玉雕龙

辽宁朝阳

5. 玉蚕蛹

6. 玉璧

7. 玉斧

8. 勾云形玉器

内蒙古敖汉旗

9. 勾云形玉器

10. 玉鸮

内蒙古赤峰

11. 勾云形玉器

1 "璋" 形玉器

Jade in the Shape of *Zhang* Tablet

于阜新福兴地镇收集
现藏阜新市博物馆
长 12.5、宽 5.5、厚 0.2 厘米
Collected at Fuxingdi, Fuxin
Collection of Fuxin Museum
L. 12.5 cm; W. 5.5 cm; T. 0.2 cm

发表于《文物》1984 年 6 期，孙守道：《红山文化玉龙考》（拓片见第
10 页图九）。

淡绿色，光泽度较高。器身扁宽而平，且甚薄。端面雕琢兽面纹，双耳
斜立，使头部呈"丫"形。有圆睛、鼻孔，以其细而浅的线雕纹围于圆
睛四周，形成面部皱折。柄部以打洼手法雕出十余道凸弦纹。尾端一角
有残缺。近尾端中央对钻单孔。

这种"璋"形器，尚未有正式考古发掘品。但其端面的双立耳、圆睛、
有皱折纹的兽面纹，十分近似于玉雕龙的展开图。同类器也见于辽宁省
文物店收藏的两件（见本书 165/166 页）。同时，此类器在端面与柄之
间都设有"栏"，牛河梁遗址出土的一件近似于这种"璋"形器的兽面
双身饰件，两侧还作出扉棱，这些都使我们与龙山时期开始出现的玉璋
产生联想。

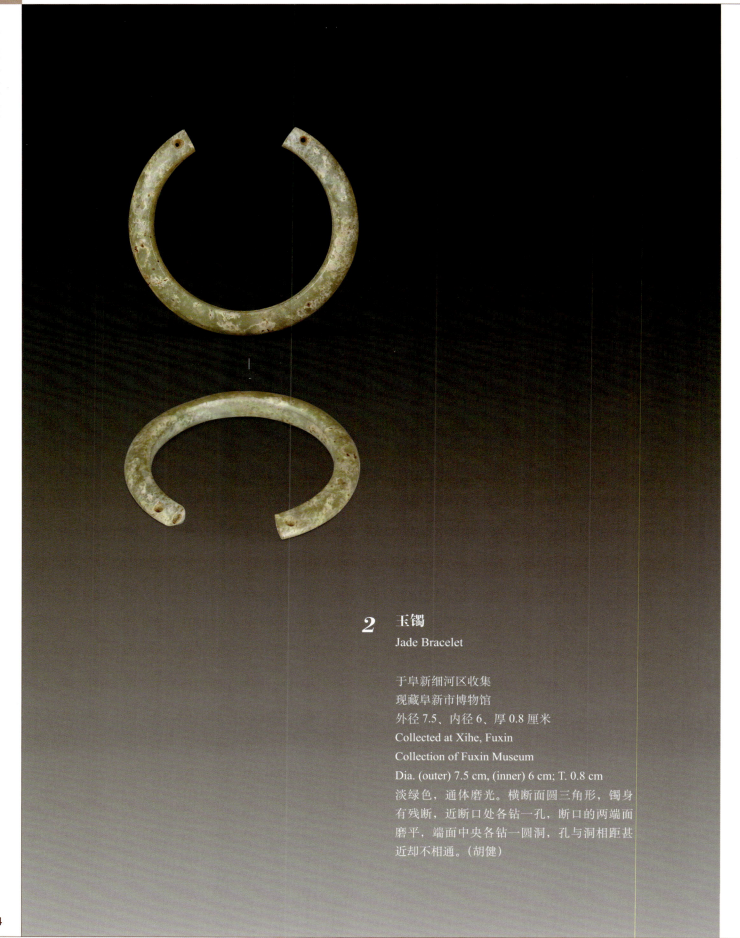

2 玉镯

Jade Bracelet

于阜新细河区收集
现藏阜新市博物馆
外径 7.5、内径 6、厚 0.8 厘米
Collected at Xihe, Fuxin
Collection of Fuxin Museum
Dia. (outer) 7.5 cm, (inner) 6 cm; T. 0.8 cm
淡绿色，通体磨光。横断面圆三角形，镯身
有残断，近断口处各钻一孔，断口的两端面
磨平，端面中央各钻一圆洞，孔与洞相距甚
近却不相通。（胡健）

3 **圭形玉器**

Jade in the Shape of *Gui* Tablet

1981 年于阜新化石戈乡收集
现藏阜新市博物馆
长 20、最宽 4、厚 0.5 厘米
Collected at Huashige, Fuxin, 1981
Collection of Fuxin Museum
L. 20 cm; W. (max) 4 cm; T. 0.5 cm
乳白色，通体磨制。扁体，顶端尖，底端磨制甚平。
此标本体形虽简洁无纹，却甚为规正。近于圭形，故名。（胡健）

4　玉雕龙

Jade Dragon

20 世纪 70 年代于建平境内征集
现藏辽宁省博物馆
高 15 厘米

Acquired in Jianping, 1970s

Collection of Museum of Liaoning Province

H. 15 cm

发表于《文物》1984 年 6 期，孙守道、郭大顺：《论辽河流域的原始文明与龙的起源》（线图见第 13 页图三，5）。
白色，质匀，通体磨光甚精，一面有大片剥蚀。环体较厚，缺口内未切断，内缘相连。大小孔都为两面钻，大孔内可见明显中脊，小孔壁则显旋纹。以流畅的阴线雕出目、口、齿及颚与吻上的皱折，其间配以减地阳纹式的瓦沟纹。有短立耳，较为宽厚。此件形体较大，整体造型十分规整，且为此类玉雕龙唯一雕有牙齿的实例。

5 玉蚕蛹（朝博2765-1）

Jade Silkworm Pupa

1990 年喀左中山家乡辘辘井村高时松捐献

现藏朝阳市博物馆

长 7、宽 2.5 厘米

Gift of Gao Shisong at Lulujing, Zhongshanjia, Kazuo, 1990

Collection of Chaoyang Museum

L. 7 cm; W. 2.5 cm

淡绿色。有较多深褐色斑。头端面平，头部五官不显，近
尾渐薄，呈下垂状，尾端圆弧。下腹面雕出三道凸弦纹为
腹节。有横竖钻孔相通，横钻孔在前部，竖钻孔从头端直
通至尾。形近那日斯台玉蚕，为简化型蚕蛹。（图片均为倒
置。尚晓波）

6 玉璧（朝博3120-考1587）

Jade *Bi* Disc

于朝阳地区征集
现藏朝阳市博物馆
直径 3.2 厘米
Acquired in Chaoyang
Collection of Chaoyang Museum
Dia. 3.2 cm

淡绿色玉，质地细腻，圆润光泽。体形较小，体扁平，
内外缘磨薄似刃，中部略鼓，外缘近于方圆形。（尚晓波）

7 玉斧（朝博1704-石37）

Jade Axe

1990 年于朝阳地区征集

现藏朝阳市博物馆

长 30.5、最宽 9 厘米

Acquired in Chaoyang, 1990

Collection of Chaoyang Museum

L. 30.5 cm; W. (max) 9 cm

黑绿色。通体琢磨，以磨制为主，表面较为光滑，有玉质天然形成的纹络。斧体较大且甚为窄长，顶端窄，两侧边有外弧，下收为弧刃，横断面为椭圆形。（尚晓波）

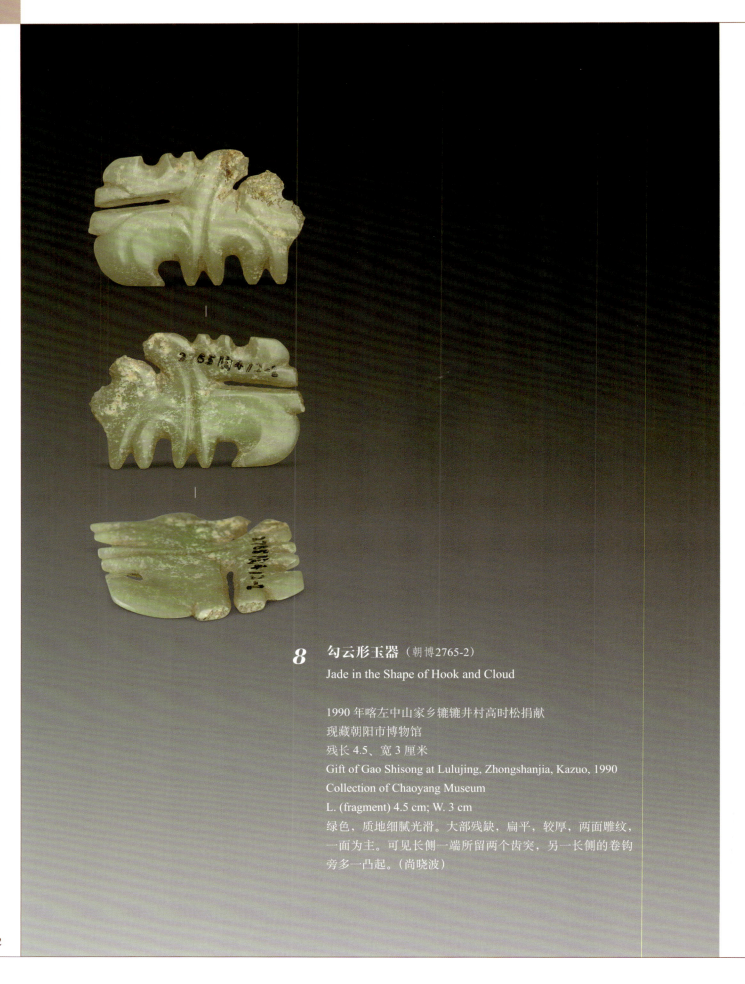

8 勾云形玉器（朝博2765-2）

Jade in the Shape of Hook and Cloud

1990 年喀左中山家乡辘辘井村高时松捐献
现藏朝阳市博物馆
残长 4.5、宽 3 厘米
Gift of Gao Shisong at Lulujing, Zhongshanjia, Kazuo, 1990
Collection of Chaoyang Museum
L. (fragment) 4.5 cm; W. 3 cm
绿色，质地细腻光滑。大部残缺，扁平、较厚，两面雕纹，
一面为主。可见长侧一端所留两个齿突，另一长侧的卷钩
旁多一凸起。（尚晓波）

9 **勾云形玉器**

Jade in the Shape of Hook and Cloud

敖汉旗征集
现藏敖汉旗博物馆
长 12、宽 4.5 厘米
Acquired at Aohan
Collection of Aohan Banner Museum
L. 12 cm; W. 4.5 cm
发表于邵国田主编：《敖汉文物精华》（第 72 页），内蒙古文化出
版社，2004 年。
色淡黄间灰白色，质细腻，有黑褐色瑕斑。体较厚而长. 长边一
侧圆弧，无卷勾的表现，并对钻单孔，另侧两端内勾，中部起三棱，
整体显示为勾云形玉器的简化。

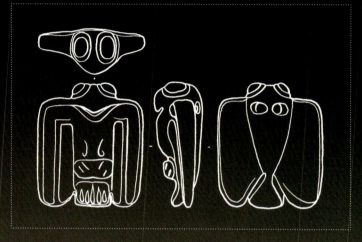

10 玉鸮

Jade Owl

于敖汉旗征集

现藏敖汉旗博物馆

高 5.4、宽 4.7、厚 2 厘米

Acquired at Aohan

Collection of Aohan Banner Museum

H. 5.4 cm; W. 4.7 cm; T. 2 cm

发表于邵国田主编：《敖汉文物精华》（第 68 页），
内蒙古文化出版社，2004 年。

黄色，有深红色斑痕。顶部双圆目突出，勾喙较短，
平肩略耸，展翅较窄而垂直，尾部也较窄而尾端较
为平直。以阴刻线表现爪与尾羽，翅羽则以起地阳
纹表现。

11 勾云形玉器

Jade in the Shape of Hook and Cloud

由赤峰市文物商店征集
现藏赤峰市文物商店
长 13、宽 9.2、厚 0.5 厘米
Acquired by Chifeng Antiquity Shop
Collection of Chifeng Antiquity Shop
L. 13 cm; W. 9.2 cm; T. 0.5 cm
发表于于建设主编:《红山玉器》(第 148 页),远方
出版社,2004 年。
淡绿色,有淡黑色瑕斑。体较薄,整体近于方形,
四角卷钩短而明确,中心卷钩与器体间隔的镂空部
分较宽,两面有纹,为中心打洼形成的随卷钩走向
而甚浅的瓦沟纹。顶部钻单孔,孔较大。

6 其他珍贵收集品
OTHER IMPORTANT COLLECTIONS

LIAONING PROVINCE

1. Coiled Jade Dragon
2. Jade Dragon Head
3. Jade Arm Ornament
4. Hoof-shaped Jades
5. Jade *Bi* Disc
6. Jade Dragon
7. Jade in the Shape of *Zhang* Tablet with Animal Mask
8. Jade in the Shape of *Zhang* Tablet with Animal Mask
9. Hook-shaped Jade
10. Hook-shaped Jade
11. Jade Owl
12. Jade Owl
13. Two-ring Jade *Bi* Disc
14. Hoof-shaped Jade
15. Jade in the Shape of Hook and Cloud
16. Jade Dragon

BEIJING

17. Jade Dragon
18. Jade in the Shape of Hook and Cloud
19. Bird-shaped Jade
20. Jade Dragon
21. Jade Dragon
22. Jade Dragon
23. Jade Owl
24. Coiled Jade Dragon
25. Jade Sitting Figure
26. Jade Human Figure Stepping on Beast
27. Hoof-shaped Jasper
28. Hoof-shaped Jade
29. Hoof-shaped Jade
30. Hoof-shaped Jade
31. Owl-shaped Jade Pendant
32. Owl-shaped Jade Pendant
33. Jade Bird
34. Jade in the Shape of Hook and Cloud
35. Jade in the Shape of Hook and Cloud
36. Jade *Huang*
37. Jade Dragon

38. Jade *Bi* Disc
39. Two-ring Jade *Bi* Disc

TIANJIN

40. Jade Owl
41. Jade in the Shape of Hook and Cloud
42. Jade in the Shape of Hook and Cloud
43. Jade in the Shape of Hook and Cloud
44. Jade Animal in the Shape of Double Gourd
45. Hoof-shaped Jade
46. Jade Dragon
47. Jade Dragon
48. Jade Dragon Head
49. Jade Dragon
50. Jade in the Shape of *Zhang* Tablet
51. Celadonish Jade Pendant in the Shape of Hook and Cloud
52. Horn-shaped Jade
53. Jade Comb Ornament with Two Snake Heads

SHANGHAI

54. Jade Owl
55. Jade Silkworm Pupa

UNITED STATES

56. Jade in the Shape of Hook and Cloud
57. Hoof-shaped Jade
58. Jade *Bi* Disc

BRITAIN

59. Jade Owl
60. Hoof-Shaped Jade
61. Hoof-Shaped Jade
62. Jade Bird
63. Jade Dragon
64. Jade Dragon

FRANCE

65. Jade Dragons

辽宁

1. 附脊玉雕龙
2. 玉雕龙首
3. 玉臂饰
4. 斜口筒形玉器
5. 玉璧
6. 玉雕龙
7. 兽面纹"璋"形玉器
8. 兽面纹"璋"形玉器
9. 钩形玉器
10. 钩形玉器
11. 玉鸮
12. 玉鸮
13. 双联玉璧
14. 斜口筒形玉器
15. 勾云形玉器
16. 玉雕龙

北京

17. 玉雕龙
18. 勾云形玉器
19. "鸟"形玉器
20. 玉雕龙
21. 玉雕龙
22. 玉雕龙
23. 玉鸮
24. 附脊玉雕龙

25. 玉坐人
26. 玉人踏兽神像
27. 斜口筒形玉器
28. 斜口筒形玉器
29. 斜口筒形玉器
30. 斜口筒形玉器
31. 玉鸮形珮
32. 玉鸮形珮
33. 玉鸟
34. 勾云形玉器
35. 勾云形玉器
36. 玉璜形器
37. 玉雕龙
38. 玉璧
39. 双联玉璧

天津

40. 玉鸮
41. 勾云形玉器
42. 勾云形玉器
43. 勾云形玉器
44. 葫芦形玉兽
45. 斜口筒形玉器
46. 玉雕龙
47. 玉雕龙
48. 玉雕龙首
49. 玉雕龙

50. "璋"形玉器
51. 勾云形玉珮
52. 角形玉器
53. 双蛇首玉梳背饰

上海

54. 玉鸮
55. 玉蚕蛹

美国

56. 勾云形玉器
57. 斜口筒形玉器
58. 玉璧

英国

59. 玉鸮
60. 斜口筒形玉器
61. 斜口筒形玉器
62. 玉鸟
63. 玉雕龙
64. 玉雕龙

法国

65. 玉雕龙

1 附脊玉雕龙

Coiled Jade Dragon

1956 年 10 月 15 日购于北京并入藏沈阳鲁迅美术学院

现藏沈阳鲁迅美术学院博物馆

通高 24.6、龙身总长（外缘）约 55、总宽 19.8、孔径 0.6~0.8 厘米，重 720 克

Purchased in Beijing, 1956

Collection of Luxun Academy of Fine Arts, Shenyang

H. 24.6 cm; L. (body) (outer) c. 55 cm; W. 19.8 cm; Dia. (perforation) 0.6 — 0.8 cm; Wt. 720 g

墨绿色玉质。体卷曲，平面形状如一"C"形，龙体横截面为椭圆形，直径 2.3×2.9 厘米。龙首较短小，吻前伸，略向上弯曲，嘴紧闭，鼻端呈弧面，端面近椭圆形，弧面上有对称的两个鼻翼和鼻孔。双眼突起呈梭形，内眼角圆面起棱，眼尾细长。额及颚底刻以细密的方格网状纹，网格突起作规整的小菱形。颈脊起一长鬣，位于龙体前三分之一处，鬣形随龙身弯曲，尾部上扬；鬣外缘长 20 厘米，内缘长 13.8 厘米；鬣为片状，内外缘打磨成刃状，两缘之间打磨出不显著的浅凹形状。龙身大部光素无纹，龙体前二分之一处有穿。

玉龙以一整块玉料圆雕而成，细部还运用了浮雕、浅浮雕等手法，通体琢磨，较为光洁。玉质有瑕和沁，鬣部有一小损伤。其余基本完整。（沈阳鲁迅美术学院博物馆）

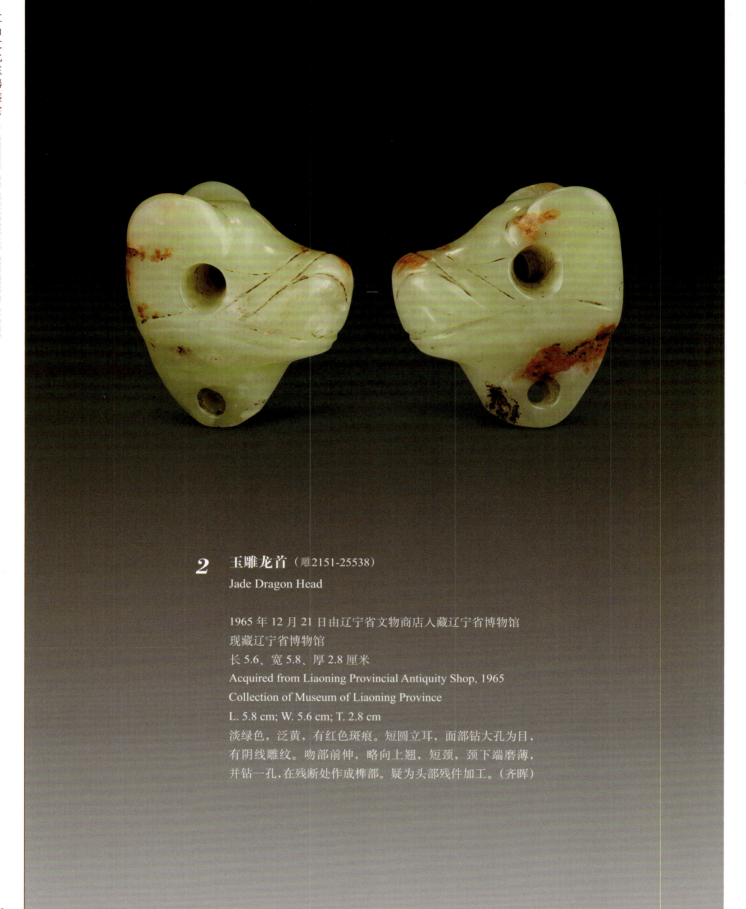

2　**玉雕龙首**（雕2151-25538）

Jade Dragon Head

1965 年 12 月 21 日由辽宁省文物商店入藏辽宁省博物馆
现藏辽宁省博物馆
长 5.6、宽 5.8、厚 2.8 厘米
Acquired from Liaoning Provincial Antiquity Shop, 1965
Collection of Museum of Liaoning Province
L. 5.8 cm; W. 5.6 cm; T. 2.8 cm
淡绿色，泛黄，有红色斑痕。短圆立耳，面部钻大孔为目，
有阴线雕纹。吻部前伸，略向上翘，短颈，颈下端磨薄，
并钻一孔，在残断处作成榫部。疑为头部残件加工。（齐晖）

3　**玉臂饰**（雕2122－25037）

Jade Arm Ornament

辽宁省博物馆旧藏
现藏辽宁省博物馆
长 10.5、宽 7.8、厚 0.5 厘米
Collection of Museum of Liaoning Province
L. 10.5 cm; W. 7.8 cm; T. 0.5 cm

淡绿色，泛黄。片状，复瓦形。一边平，
近边缘钻等距三孔，另边作成双弧线状。
外表饰瓦沟纹，呈规整的"回"字形，内
壁遗有较宽的线切割痕。

该器物应该是作为装饰物系绳加固在手臂
之上，也有人认为与北方民族饲养鹰类动
物的传统有关。（齐晖）

4 **斜口筒形玉器**（雕2122-25037）

Hoof-shaped Jades

1963 年 11 月 5 日入藏辽宁省博物馆

现藏辽宁省博物馆

高 4.8 、径 8.1 厘米

高 4.6 、径 8.1 厘米

Collection of Museum of Liaoning Province

H. 4.8 cm; Dia. 8.1 cm

H. 4.6 cm; Dia. 8.1 cm

2 件。一只残件，一只斜口部分疑为后改制。

暗绿色软玉磨制。此类玉器形制简略，多呈椭圆形筒状，筒体一端作斜面，另一端平，外表光素无纹。出土时大都横置于人头下，个别置于腰部右侧。对其用途有多种猜测，如为铲土工具、套在臂上的臂饰、束发器、通神的礼器、祭祀占卜器等。

据李文信先生口述，此器原系热河出土，伪满奉天博物馆藏，抗日战争胜利后遗失。辗转多年，后由辽宁省文物商店收购，并入藏辽宁省博物馆。（齐晖）

5 玉璧（雕2703-30386）

Jade *Bi* Disc

1990 年辽宁省文物商店收购

现藏辽宁省博物馆

直径 7.05、厚 0.5 厘米

Purchased by Liaoning Provincial Antiquity Shop, 1990

Collection of Museum of Liaoning Province

Dia. 7.05 cm; T. 0.5 cm

方圆形，即玉璧的孔缘近圆形，而玉璧的外轮廓往往做成方圆形，甚至接近正方形。内外缘皆不起棱边，而是加工成薄似刀刃的状态，显示了红山人制玉技术的成熟。其外缘方，内孔圆，内外边薄似刃，方圆结合可能反映了红山人天圆地方的观念。（齐晖）

6　玉雕龙
Jade Dragon

原藏辽宁省文物总店
高 4.2、宽 3.4、厚 1.4 厘米
Fromer Liaoning Provincial Antiquity Shop
H. 4.2 cm; W. 3.4 cm; T. 1.4 cm
发表于《文物》1984 年 6 期,孙守道:《红山文化玉龙考》(线图见第 10 页图七)。
褐色玉,体较小而细。首似猪,圆眼,大耳,首部有数道压缩回旋状五官刻线,吻部前凸,颈部有一小圆穿孔,周身光素。
这类玉雕龙,形体较小,头部小而体较细。同类器还见于旅顺博物馆收藏的一件(见本书 173 页)。黄濬《古玉图录初集》(1939 年)也收录一件。(孙亭、程秀岩)

7 **兽面纹"璋"形玉器**（4-1017．2）

Jade in the Shape of *Zhang* Tablet with Animal Mask

20 世纪 80 年代初或前收购
现藏辽宁省文物总店
长 15.2、宽 2.8、厚 0.35 厘米
Purchased in or prior to the early 1980s
Collection of Liaoning Provincial Antiquity Shop
L. 15.2 cm; W. 2.8 cm; T. 0.35 cm

发表于《辽海文物学刊》1994 年 2 期，程秀岩：《辽宁省文物总
店藏红山文化玉器》（线图见第 133 页图四左）。

深绿色，中部一面有大片黄色瑕斑及裂纹。长条板状，甚为扁平。
形同福兴地收集的一件（见本书 142 页）而体甚细长，首部刻纹
已不显，似为出土后长期磨损所为。圆睛不规则，短圆弧线相接
成睛的作法更为明显。有对称双鼻孔。体饰弦纹较宽且较深，使
两侧边缘也起与弦纹对应的棱线。近底部中央对钻单孔。（孙亭、
程秀岩）

8

9

9 钩形玉器（4-162）
Hook-shaped Jade

20 世纪 70 年代收购
现藏辽宁省文物总店
长 9.5、宽 3.1 厘米
Purchased in the 1970s
Collection of Liaoning Provincial Antiquity Shop
L. 9.5 cm; W. 3.1 cm

发表于《辽海文物学刊》1994 年 2 期，程秀岩：《辽宁省文物总店藏红山文化玉器》（线图见第 133 页图五左）

淡绿色，泛黄，有淡褐色瑕斑，较光泽，通体磨光。扁体，分钩形体、栏和柄三部分，钩形体较宽，边起棱线，栏起双棱，间隔较宽，直柄下端做出榫状，榫面穿一小孔。侧边、柄、栏有内外压地起棱的作法。（孙亭、程秀岩）

8 兽面纹"璋"形玉器（4-1017．1）
Jade in the Shape of *Zhang* Tablet with Animal Mask

20 世纪 80 年代初或前收购
现藏辽宁省文物总店
长 12.4、宽 4.1、厚 0.2 厘米
Purchased in or prior to the early 1980s
Collection of Liaoning Provincial Antiquity Shop
L. 12.4 cm; W. 4.1 cm; T. 0.2 cm

发表于《辽海文物学刊》1994 年 2 期，程秀岩：《辽宁省文物总店藏红山文化玉器》（线图见第 133 页图四右）。

淡黄色，近底边有褐色瑕斑。近底端两侧有残。长条形，甚为平整。可分为首与扁体两部分，中有栏相隔。首端雕兽面纹。耳斜立呈"Y"形，圆睛以短弧线形阴刻线相交连接而成。睛的周围有多道甚浅而细的阴刻纹环绕，睛下显甚小的双圆洞，应为鼻孔。栏内有槽，槽两端宽，端也钻甚小的圆洞。器体边缘磨薄，体的一面磨出多道弦纹，另面平而无纹。尾端磨薄似榫，近尾端中央对钻甚小的单孔。（孙亭、程秀岩）

10　钩形玉器

Hook-shaped Jade

20 世纪 80 年代初或前收购

现藏辽宁省文物总店

长 9.5、宽 2 厘米

Purchased in or prior to the early 1980s

Collection of Liaoning Provincial Antiquity Shop

L. 9.5 cm; W. 2 cm

发表于《辽海文物学刊》1994 年 2 期，程秀岩：《辽宁省文物总店藏红山文化玉器》（线图见第 166 页图五右）。

淡绿色，泛黄褐色，柄部间有褐红色瑕斑。形近前件（见本书 166 页），唯器身甚为窄长，弯度较大。柄也较为细长，榫部较短。榫面上对钻的单孔较大。钩体面上有中部压地形成的外起阳纹斜边的做法。

玉钩形器还见于那日斯台遗址。辽宁省文物总店收藏的两件，柄均较长，榫也更加明确，应为复合器。（孙亭、程秀岩）

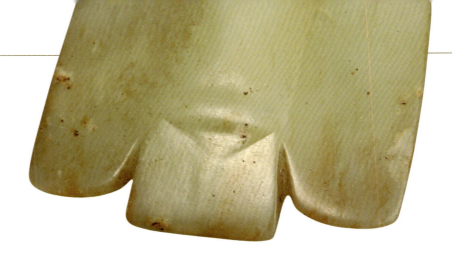

11 玉鸮（4-1093）

Jade Owl

20 世纪 80 年代初或前收购

现藏辽宁省文物总店

长 4.8、宽 4.9 厘米

Purchased in or prior to the early 1980s

Collection of Liaoning Provincial Antiquity Shop

L. 4.8 cm; W. 4.9 cm

发表于《辽海文物学刊》1994 年 2 期，程秀岩：《辽宁省文物总店藏红山文化玉器》（线图见第 133 页图六右）。

浅黄色，局部微显淡褐色。圆肩，方尾，双翼边缘稍显外弧形。前厚后薄，上腹部尤鼓，由中腹部向尾及双翅磨出斜面，近尾及翅边磨薄，侧面视翅与尾略有上翘，形成展翅飞翔的效果。正面用细线雕出首部，尾部、双翅、头部圆厚，头顶面雕出微鼓的圆睛，睛周有细线围绕。头下磨出深槽与腹部相隔。下腹正中隐约可见鸟爪。两翅面磨平，翅羽以中间凸起一竖行阳纹表现，此阳纹甚细而浅直，背面横钻一隧孔，孔的位置近于头部。（孙亭、程秀岩）

12　玉鸮 (4-12191)
Jade Owl

20 世纪 80 年代初或前收购
现藏辽宁省文物总店
长 5、宽 4.5 厘米
Purchased in or prior to the early 1980s
Collection of Liaoning Provincial Antiquity Shop
L. 5 cm; W. 4.5 cm

发表于《辽海文物学刊》1994 年 2 期，程秀岩：《辽宁省文物总店藏红山文化玉器》（线图见第 133 页图六左）。

深绿色，正面有淡黄褐色斑纹，近边缘泛黄色。肩稍显圆鼓上耸，展翅内收，翅尾尖。尾端稍圆。顶面有微凸的圆睛，腹鼓，背面两翅及近尾部磨出斜面，翅及尾边薄，使双翅及尾部稍上翘，显飞翔状。双翅面显内凹，中部凸起一道较粗的阳线，以表现翅羽。背面有竖钻的单隧孔。（孙亭、程秀岩）

13 **双联玉璧**（4-1115）

Two-ring Jade *Bi* Disc

20 世纪 80 年代初或前收购
现藏辽宁省文物总店
长 9.5、宽 4.5 厘米
Purchased in or prior to the early 1980s
Collection of Liaoning Provincial Antiquity Shop
L. 9.5 cm; W. 4.5 cm
发表于辽宁省文物店编：《汲古丛珍》（图版 186），文物出
版社，1997 年。
淡绿色，色甚浅且泛黄，有淡色斑及裂纹。似双璧相连，
内外边均磨薄，双孔皆对钻。二璧形状、大小相同，都为
圆三角形，外侧两端各有饰物，似为起牙。有以为是蚕的
形象。（孙亭、程秀岩）

14 斜口筒形玉器

Hoof-shaped Jade

20 世纪 70 年代前后收购
现藏辽宁省文物总店
高 8、口径 7、下口径 8 厘米
Purchased around the 1970s
Collection of Liaoning Provincial Antiquity Shop
H. 8 cm; Dia. (top) 7 cm, (bottom) 8 cm

发表于《辽海文物学刊》1994 年 2 期，程秀岩：《辽宁省文物总店藏红山文化玉器》（线图见第 132 页图三）。深绿色。一侧有成片黄褐片状瑕斑。近平口的外侧有残凹坑。扁圆筒状。斜口部分残断，断面边缘磨平。可见内壁线切割纹，平口内侧边有斜刻的短槽一周。长面壁较厚，平口一侧有对称钻孔，以由外向内钻为主。钻孔位置偏于长面一侧。此件斜口筒形玉器虽然残断后加工，但可明显看出长面较厚而短面较薄，这同龟壳背甲较厚腹甲较薄的特征相同，而钻孔在长面一侧，也同史前时期所出龟壳钻孔以背甲为主的现象相近，是斜口筒形玉器为龟壳的进一步证据。

15 勾云形玉器

Jade in the Shape of Hook and Cloud

20 世纪 70 年代前后收购

现藏辽宁省文物总店

长 11.3、宽 8.9、厚 0.35 厘米

Purchased around the 1970s

Collection of Liaoning Provincial Antiquity Shop

L. 11.3 cm; W. 8.9 cm; T. 0.35 cm

发表于《辽海文物学刊》1994 年 2 期，程秀岩：《辽宁省文物总店藏红山文化玉器》（线图见第 132 页图二）。

青灰间青黑色，一侧色深。扁平体。有正、反面之分。反面甚平而不施纹。正面瓦沟纹较宽而深。中央镂空作勾云状盘卷，四角伸出勾卷角，器中间部位稍厚，边缘稍薄，刃部较锋利。器面研磨出与形制相适应的浅凹槽，器的一角稍有残，长侧上部有对穿的双孔，钻孔前先刻出横斜的短槽，且为先施瓦沟纹后钻孔。（孙亭、程秀岩）

6

16 玉雕龙

Jade Dragon

旅顺博物馆旧藏

现藏旅顺博物馆

高 6.7、宽 5.5、厚 2.3 厘米

Collection of Lüshun Museum

H. 6.7 cm; W. 5.5 cm; T. 2.3 cm

淡绿色，有白斑。龙体卷曲呈"C"形，首尾相隔而对，尾圆尖平齐。两耳较大为半圆形（一耳微残），双目圆睁，眼窝深陷，吻部前伸，鼻微上翘刻有褶皱，嘴微启，颈有对钻圆孔。龙体丰圆，琢磨精细，造型古朴，为红山文化玉器——玦形玉龙类的典型器。

该玉器是旅顺博物馆建馆初期的藏品，故也称"旧藏"，据传1920年代出土于辽西地区。著录于1933年刊行的《关东厅博物馆考古图录》和1940年刊行的《旅顺博物馆陈列品图录》，时代定为"汉及汉以前时代"，并笼统称为"支那发现品"。（王嗣洲）

17 玉雕龙

Jade Dragon

传世品
现藏首都博物馆
高 16、宽 11、内径 2.7、厚 2.3 厘米
Handed down
Collection of Capital Museum
H. 16 cm; W. 11 cm; Dia. (inner) 2.7 cm; T. 2.3 cm

头尾相接明显，耳不耸立，吻有前伸，面部雕
纹浅而匀。尤其是环体及中心大孔、背双孔甚
至眼睛，皆呈椭圆形，在同类玉雕龙中是体态
较有特点的标本。

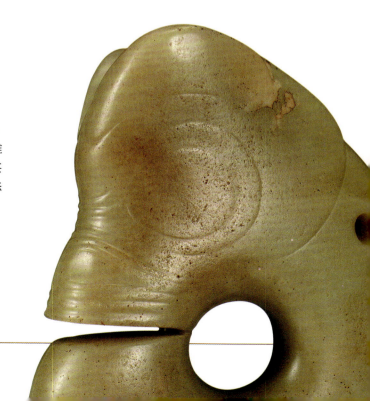

18

18　勾云形玉器

Jade in the Shape of Hook and Cloud

颐和园旧藏
现藏首都博物馆
长 11.8、宽 6.4 厘米
Formerly collected by Summer Palace
Collection of Capital Museum
L. 11.8 cm; W. 6.4 cm

一角残缺，器面饰纹不显。四角卷钩外凸明显，
二中心卷钩对向分布，是单钩形勾云形玉器结
合而成双钩形勾云形玉器的又一实证。

19

19　"鸟"形玉器

Bird-shaped Jade

传世品
现藏首都博物馆
长 9.1、宽 4.3 厘米
Handed down
Collection of Capital Museum
L. 9.1 cm; W. 4.3 cm

长板状。一端有反向卷钩，另端依次呈圆弧形，
面上刻线既随卷钩走向，又有纵横相间，造
型应与勾云形玉器有关。

20   玉雕龙（故103952）

Jade Dragon

清宫旧藏

现藏故宫博物院

高 15.4、宽 4.5 厘米

Formerly collected by Qing royal house

Collection of the Palace Museum

H. 15.4 cm; W. 4.5 cm

发表于张广文主编：《故宫博物院藏文物珍品大系·玉器
（上）》（第 2 页图 1），上海科学技术出版社，2008 年。

青绿色。有褐色斑。环形，一侧似断开，另侧相连。断口
一侧似兽首，大耳、鼻、眼皆用粗阴线表示，兽头之下为
素环，以示兽身卷屈呈环状，兽之颈部有并排两孔。

21 **玉雕龙**（新156776）

Jade Dragon

1965 年故宫博物院收购
现藏故宫博物院
高 12、宽 7.6、厚 4.2 厘米
Purchased by Palace Museum in 1965
Collection of Palace Museum
H. 12cm; W. 7.6cm; T. 4.2cm

发表于周南泉主编《故宫博物院藏文物珍品全集·玉器（上）》，
生活·读书·新知三联书店、商务印书馆，1996 年。

玉料青绿色，局部有白色的沁斑，还有铁褐色沁斑，边缘有籽料边皮痕迹，
可能当时是根据玉料大小设计的。中部大圆孔，两面对钻，外口较大，耳后
有对钻小圆孔，为系挂孔。以片切割开玦口，玦口全开，口部较为平直。龙
首大眼，大耳竖立，鼻与嘴部前凸，饰多道弦纹，形体也较粗大。（徐琳）

22 **玉雕龙**（新178369）

Jade Dragon

1973 年故宫博物院收购

现藏故宫博物院

高 5.9、宽 4.4、厚 0.5 厘米

Purchased by Palace Museum in 1973

Collection of Palace Museum

H. 5.9cm; W. 4.4cm; T. 0.5cm

发表于周南泉主编：《故宫博物院藏文物珍品全集·玉器（上）》

生活·读书·新知三联书店、商务印书馆，1996 年。

玉料青绿色，局部有白色的沁斑。中部大圆孔，背部开小孔靠上，近头部。以片切割开玦口。龙首大眼圆凸，吻部有较深的沟纹。此龙反面扁平，留有切割痕，当为被后世切割改制。

其形体特征与常见红山玉玦形龙稍有不同，圆凸的双眼尤为明显，入藏故宫博物院时因时代辨别不准，将其归为商代玉器，但同时也认为受红山文化影响，风格不同于商代玉玦，或与红山玉器有继承之处。随着红山文化考古调查资料的丰富，我们看到了，在内蒙古敖汉旗萨力巴乡干饭营子及辽宁西部等多处出土或征集到的这类圆眼外凸的玉玦形龙，从而确定其为红山文化玉器。（徐琳）

23　玉鹗（故84717）

Jade Owl

清宫旧藏
现藏故宫博物院
高 4.6、厚 0.4 厘米
Formerly collected by Qing royal house
Collection of the Palace Museum
H.4.6 cm; T. 0.4 cm
发表于张广文主编：《故宫博物院藏文物珍品大系·玉器
（上）》（第 3 页图 3），上海科学技术出版社，2008 年。
此器因宫内失火时被烧烤，呈黑、灰色。方形，腹部较厚，
翅部有纵向的条纹，背部有钻孔时留下的痕迹。

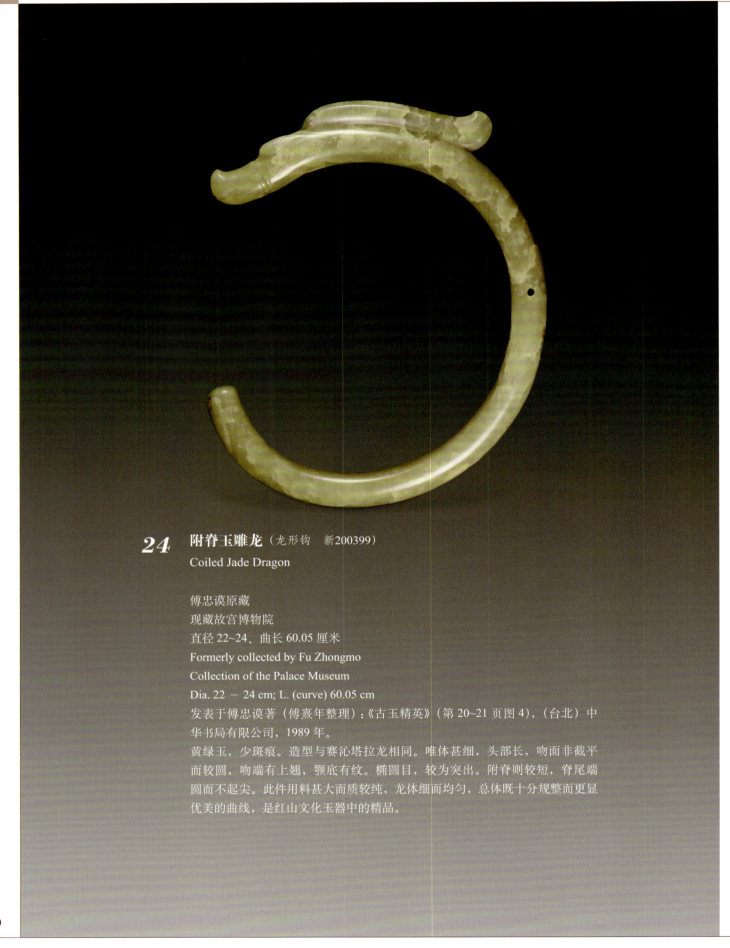

24　**附脊玉雕龙**（龙形钩　新200399）
Coiled Jade Dragon

傅忠谟原藏
现藏故宫博物院
直径 22~24、曲长 60.05 厘米
Formerly collected by Fu Zhongmo
Collection of the Palace Museum
Dia. 22 — 24 cm; L. (curve) 60.05 cm

发表于傅忠谟著（傅熹年整理）:《古玉精英》（第20~21 页图4），（台北）中
华书局有限公司，1989 年。

黄绿玉，少斑痕。造型与赛沁塔拉龙相同。唯体甚细，头部长，吻面非截平
而较圆，吻端有上翘，颚底有纹。椭圆目，较为突出。附脊则较短，脊尾端
圆而不起尖。此件用料甚大而质较纯，龙体细而均匀，总体既十分规整而更显
优美的曲线，是红山文化玉器中的精品。

25　玉坐人（新194773）

Jade Sitting Figure

1983 年初于来北京的内蒙古牧民处收购

现藏故宫博物院

高 14.6、宽 6、厚 4.7 厘米

Purchased from Inner Mongolian herdsman in Beijing, 1983

Collection of the Palace Museum

H. 14.6 cm; W. 6 cm; T. 4.7 cm

发表于张广文主编：《故宫博物院藏文物珍品大系·玉器（上）》（第 18 页图 17），上海科学技术出版社，2008 年。又见徐琳：《三尊"红山玉人"像解析》，中国社会科学报，2010 年 2 月 2 日，博物版。

青黄色，微透光，局部有玉璞皮色及大块赭色斑。有耳有角，头顶的双角高耸，角间头顶部有浅网格纹，面部窄而前凸，长耳，陷鼻，细腰，长腿，上肢短而粗，坐姿。颈背部有较大的对穿孔。曾以为是多种动物与人体的组合，现以为是带动物冠的人坐像，此动物或即鹿类。尚隐约可见人的眼睛，人目以上为人所戴兽冠的大圆凸眼。肥硕的腿部则与东山嘴遗址所出孕妇小雕像有所接近，可推测为一女性雕像。

同类器又见资料部分 27、28、29。此类玉人，尚无正式出土实例。其玉料近于红山文化常见玉料，特别值得注意的是，此类玉人倚坐式的姿态同于东山嘴遗址孕妇陶塑像，有的应另有依托物。披戴兽冠兽皮（熊及其他兽类）也与东北及东北亚渔猎人的习俗有密切联系。人披兽冠兽皮，应是巫者（萨满）作法时的装束，这同牛河梁遗址第十六地点所出玉人平卧、曲肘抚胸、吸气以上下贯通的作法姿态有所不同，可能反映通神过程中的不同程序和不同功能。

26 玉人踏兽神像（新152404）

Jade Human Figure Stepping on Beast

20 世纪 60 年代初由天津辗转到北京

1963 年入藏故宫博物院

现藏故宫博物院

高 27.7、最宽 11.7 厘米

Transferred to Beijing from Tianjin in the early 1960s

Collected by Palace Museum in 1963

Collection of Palace Museum

H. 27.7cm; W. (max) 11.7cm

发表于周南泉主编：《故宫博物院藏文物珍品全集·玉器（上）》，生活·读书·新知三联书店、商务印书馆，1996 年；孙守道：《红山文化玉祖神考》，《中国文物世界》总一五四期，1998 年 6 月号；徐琳：《玉人的启示——故宫博物院藏红山玉人像考辨》，《玉魂国魄——中国古代玉器与传统文化学术讨论会文集（四）》，浙江古籍出版社，2010 年。

青绿色玉质，背面有土斑胶着于玉器之上。整体近似长方形，中部厚，正面略呈微弧形，边缘较薄，并有一定的钝刃感。整器部分镂雕，由一人和一兽复合而成，上人下兽。神人头带勾云形高冠，身体两侧围绕着云形装饰，五官鲜明，三角形鼻凸出，身穿服饰，服饰臂膊部分及后背上饰以网格纹。神人双手合于胸前，手持一长杖形物，赤脚踏一弧形角状物。角状物下有一兽，兽似熊，伏卧，双前足前伸。此器背面是正面纹饰的反面，饰有网格纹和瓦沟状勾云纹。

玉人虽然造型、纹饰复杂，但是其制作工艺及细部纹饰特征，均不出东北史前玉器风格范畴，与近年考古发掘的红山文化玉器有许多相似之处，加之入藏较早，越来越多的证据显示其可能为红山文化玉器，时间可能在红山文化晚期。只是这件玉人的构图复杂性前所未有，可能是目前所见红山文化中等级最高的玉器，可以说它是红山玉器研究乃至史前玉器研究的重要补充，也是我们研究史前文化的一个重要参考。（徐琳）

27　**斜口筒形玉器**（新51589）

Hoof-shaped Jasper

琉璃厂古玩商岳彬原藏
20世纪50年代由文化部文物局调拨故宫博物院
现藏故宫博物院
高17.3、上宽10.2、下宽7.8、壁厚0.3厘米
Formerly collected by Yue Bin, an antique dealer of
Liulichang
Transferred to Palace Museum by State Administration of
Cultural Heritage in the 1950s
Collection of Palace Museum, Beijing
H. 17.3cm; W. (top) 10.2cm; W. (bottom) 7.8cm; T. 0.3cm

发表于徐琳主编：《山川菁英——中国与墨西哥古代玉
石文明》，紫禁城出版社，2012年。

墨绿色玉质，玉中有黑点。体扁筒形，上端斜口，下
端平口。器内壁为先钻孔，再进行线切割，有钻孔及
线切割留下的痕迹。

类似玉器在辽宁牛河梁红山文化遗址中已发现多件，
也有因其形似马蹄，称之为马蹄形器者。出土时或放
置于人头骨上、下，或放置于胸腹间或右肩部。关于
其用途，有多种说法，如发饰、工具等等，但从最新
的考古发现看，其可能受到安徽凌家滩文化玉龟形器
的影响，是祭祀或敬神仪式中占筮的法器。（徐琳）

28 **斜口筒形玉器**（新969610）

Hoof-shaped Jade

20 世纪 50 年代进入故宫博物院

现藏故宫博物院

高 9.5、上口径 9×7.1、下口径 6.9×5.5 厘米

Collected by Palace Museum in the 1950s

Collection of Palace Museum, Beijing

H. 9.5cm; Dia. (top) (long) 9cm; (short) 7.1cm;

Dia. (bottom) (long) 6.9cm, (short) 5.5cm

发表于周南泉主编：《故宫博物院藏文物珍品全集·玉器(上)》，生活·读书·新知三联书店、商务印书馆，1996 年。

青绿色玉质，下端有土褐色沁斑，内外壁打磨光滑。整体呈扁圆筒状，上端斜口，下端平口。两侧没有穿孔。

类似玉器在辽宁牛河梁红山文化遗址中已发现多件，对其用途多有争议，但据 2007 年安徽凌家滩 23 号墓发现的玉龟形器来看，此类玉器的造型和凌家滩文化玉龟形器有很多类似之处，可能受到凌家滩文化的影响，原是祭祀或敬神仪式中占筮的法器。（徐琳）

29 **斜口筒形玉器**（新111962）
Hoof-shaped Jade

琉璃厂古玩商倪玉书原藏
20 世纪 50 年代由北京市文化局调拨故宫博物院
现藏故宫博物院
高 9.9、口径 7.8×6.6 厘米
Formerly collected by Ni Yushu, an antique dealer of Liulichang
Transferred to Palace Museum by Beijing Cultural Bureau in the 1950s
Collection of Palace Museum
H. 9.9cm；Dia. (long) 7.8cm, (short) 6.6cm
发表于张广文主编：《故宫博物院文物藏品大系·玉器（1）》，紫禁
城出版社，2011 年。
青绿色玉质。整器呈扁圆筒状，下部口沿处有缺口。上口沿及下口
沿均有绳切割留下的痕迹，为典型的红山文化玉器。（徐琳）

30　**斜口筒形玉器**（新178421）

Hoof-shaped Jade

现藏故宫博物院
高 11.7、宽 9.3、厚 0.69 厘米
Collection of the Palace Museum
H. 11.7 cm; W. 9.3 cm; T. 0.69 cm
发表于张广文主编：《故宫博物院藏文物珍品大系·玉器（上）》（第 6 页图 5），上海科学技术出版社，2008 年。
青绿色，有褐色斑。筒状，截面椭圆形，一端较粗，另一端两侧有孔，筒内壁有较多的弧形切割线，有钻孔时留下的钻痕。

31 **玉鹗形佩** （新200401）

Owl-shaped Jade Pendant

傅忠谟原藏

1992 年故宫博物院收购

现藏故宫博物院

高 3.7 厘米、宽 3.5 厘米、厚 1.3 厘米

Formerly collected by Fu Zhongmo

Purchased by Palace Museum in 1992

Collection of the Palace Museum

H. 3.7 cm; W. 3.5 cm; T. 1.3cm

发表于傅忠谟著（傅熹年整理）：《古玉精英》

（图版6），(台北)中华书局有限公司，1989 年。

黄绿色玉，鹗首为三角形，双爪抱于胸前，

圆形目斜磨，较为独特的是下尾部有一钻孔，

呈喇叭形。因背面原有对穿隧孔，后残缺磨

掉，所以可能原用背后穿孔因后残缺，改为

尾部穿孔。

此物表现的是双翼微后掠的滑翔姿态，因两

爪收于胸前，傅忠谟先生认为是鹰，但笔者

细看发现，应为鹗，但其和展翅之玉鹗完全

不同，应还是一种收翅的状态。此玉身上所

有雕琢之处均打磨得十分圆滑，若有若无，

有一种含蓄之美。（徐琳）

32　**玉鸮形珮**（新116124）

Owl-shaped Jade Pendant

琉璃厂古玩商倪玉书原藏

1959 年代由北京市文化局调拨故宫博物院

现藏故宫博物院

高 2.5、宽 4.6、厚 0.4 厘米

Formerly collected by Ni Yushu, an antique dealer of Liulichang

Transferred to Palace Museum by Beijing Cultural Bureau in 1959

Collection of Palace Museum

H. 2.5cm; W. 4.6cm; T. 0.4cm

发表于周南泉主编：《故宫博物院藏文物珍品全集・玉器（上）》生活・读书・新知三联书店、商务印书馆，1996 年；徐琳：《故宫藏红山文化动物形玉及人形玉探讨》，中国社会科学院考古研究所公共考古中心等编著《玉文化论丛（4）・红山文化专号》，众志美术出版社，2011 年。

青绿色玉料，器身有土褐色沁斑。玉鸮呈展翅状，正面琢出头和尖嘴，双翅与尾部有数道较粗的阴刻线表示羽纹。背面虽光素无纹，但有实心钻对穿的隧孔，上部对穿后，中间穿鼻残断，又从下面重新打一隧孔，孔内残留有一圈圈的钻孔痕和磨损痕，由此看出此玉鸮当时曾被长期佩戴。其造型与辽宁阜新胡头沟墓地 1 号墓出土的一件玉鸮相似，可证为红山文化玉器。（徐琳）

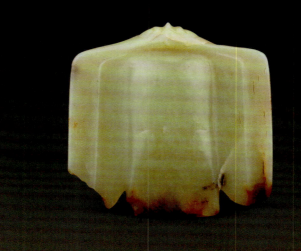

33 玉鸟（新43041）

Jade Bird

现藏故宫博物院

高 2.5、宽 4.6、厚 0.4 厘米

Collection of the Palace Museum

H. 2.5 cm; W. 4.6 cm; T. 0.4 cm

发表于张广文主编：《故宫博物院藏文物珍品大系·玉器（上）》（第
3 页图 2），上海科学技术出版社，2008 年。

青黄色，微透光，局部有红斑，似为朱砂染色。片状，边缘处略薄。

鹰头较小，展翅状，翅尾刻阴线以示羽，足爪于胸前。

红山文化玉器，偶见有器上附朱砂的，如资料部分 6-22，推测为
红山文化玉器遗于商周时期墓葬时所为。

34 **勾云形玉器**（镂雕勾云形玉珮　新200400）

Jade in the Shape of Hook and Cloud

傅忠谟原藏
1992 年故宫博物院收购
现藏故宫博物院
高 6.4、长 13.7、厚 0.75 厘米
Formerly collected by Fu Zhongmo
Purchased by Palace Museum in 1992
Collection of the Palace Museum
H. 6.74cm; W. 13.57cm; T. 0.75cm

发表于傅忠谟著（傅熹年整理）:《古玉精英》（图版 7）,（台北）中华书局有限公司, 1989 年。

黄绿色玉质，玉中有糖色。整器呈长方形片状，镂雕一正一反两个卷云状单钩。四边有卷钩形齿牙，上部中间有一穿孔，上端有二凸齿，下边有一对齿牙，整体线条的两面均磨出瓦沟纹，边缘较薄，呈刃状。这件勾云形器似为两个单勾云形组合而成，与一般红山文化出土的勾云形器略有不同，但还应归属于勾云形器的范畴。

目前学术界对红山文化勾云形器的造型、功能以及象征意义有过多种解释，笔者认为此类勾云形器无兽面眼和成组牙齿，与另一类带齿动物面纹饰相似，但玉雕主题的侧重点不同并有所区别。此类玉器有着十分明确的象征意义，那就是对天空中云的模拟，在红山人眼中它们就象征着云，云能带来雨，这也正是北方农牧业在干旱气候中十分需要的。在无任何科学知识解释的时代下，云带给红山人的遐想是最多的，也是最神秘的。勾云形珮的大量出现应该是对云的膜拜，对雨的祈求，对天的敬畏。(徐琳)

35 勾云形玉器（新141648）

Jade in the Shape of Hook and Cloud

1954 年故宫博物院收购

现藏故宫博物院

高 8.3、宽 4.9、厚 0.3 厘米

Purchased by Palace Museum in 1954

Collection of the Palace Museum

H.8.3cm; W.4.9cm; T.0.3cm

发表于周南泉主编：《故宫博物院藏文物珍品全集·玉器（上）》，生活·读书·新知三联书店、商务印书馆，1996 年。

玉已受沁为鸡骨白色，下部有三对齿牙。本定名为玉梳，但仔细观察，其与巴林右旗博物馆所藏的查干诺尔苏木出土的一件勾云形器十分类似，只是残缺了一半，故原应是一件红山文化带齿动物面纹勾云形器。对于这类玉器所代表的形象，有多种解释：有些认为是抽象的饕餮纹，有些认为是鹰面或鸟面，还有认为是猪面或兽面。笔者认为，动物面纹玉饰在史前各文化区中多有发现，大多是一种非特定动物的造型，它们应该是先民们从自己身边最常见或最害怕的一种动物或几种动物集合抽象而来的具有神话性质的动物，因神秘而敬畏，并神话为本族的保护神，将其雕刻成器成为奉神之礼，或佩挂于身成为保护之神，此时，有象征动物的眼睛和象征威力的牙齿已经足矣，动物本身为何物已不再重要。重要的是，不管红山文化这类器物代表何种动物，其两侧都有勾云相伴，这就像故宫博物院所藏玉人兽神像身边缭绕的云纹一样，勾云在这里成为它们升天的指示，是天空的象征，动物有云的环绕，也有了升入天空的神性，所以，云与动物或人物的组合，明显都有助于他们升天，都是他们升天的一种借力和象征性的道具。红山人对天的膜拜，是通过在重要的玉器上加刻云纹表现的。（徐琳）

36 玉璜形器（故95791）

Jade *Huang*

清宫旧藏
现藏故宫博物院
高 20.2、宽 12.5、厚 0.7 厘米
Formerly collected by Qing royal house
Collection of the Palace Museum
H. 20.2 cm; W. 12.5 cm; T. 0.7cm

发表于徐琳：《玉人的启示——故宫博物院藏红山玉人像考辨》，《玉魂国魄——中国古代玉器与传统文化学术讨论会文集（四）》，浙江古籍出版社，2010 年。

黄绿色玉，有微红褐色沁。玉身上靠中线处有一道随形圆弧的脊线，浅浅磨出。整器中间略厚，四边较薄呈刃状，两侧呈花叶边形弧。下部有一个插榫形的出脊，侧边打有两孔，正中一大孔，上面有极细阴刻线花纹，角两头上卷并钻孔，所有打孔都是两面对钻的实心钻斜孔。此玉外轮廓及钻孔处有后改制痕迹，从玉质及玉中间所磨出的脊线看，具有红山玉器的风格，但这类玉器还未见考古出土品，因此对确认其文化归属及功能带来了一定难度。从其造型看，此器类似角形器（故亦可称角形器），联系故宫博物院所藏玉座人头上所带的角形器，还有故宫博物院所藏玉人兽神像中玉人赤脚所站的角形器，以及英国剑桥大学所藏玉人脚下所踩踏的角状物看，笔者认为，这可能是红山文化一个具有象征性的图像符号，其造型来源于动物之角，可能是红山大巫或首领借助升天的脚力象征。

器身上的花纹当为清代加刻，同时配了紫檀木座，木座之上还镶嵌一块明代的玉螭龙形珮。（徐琳）

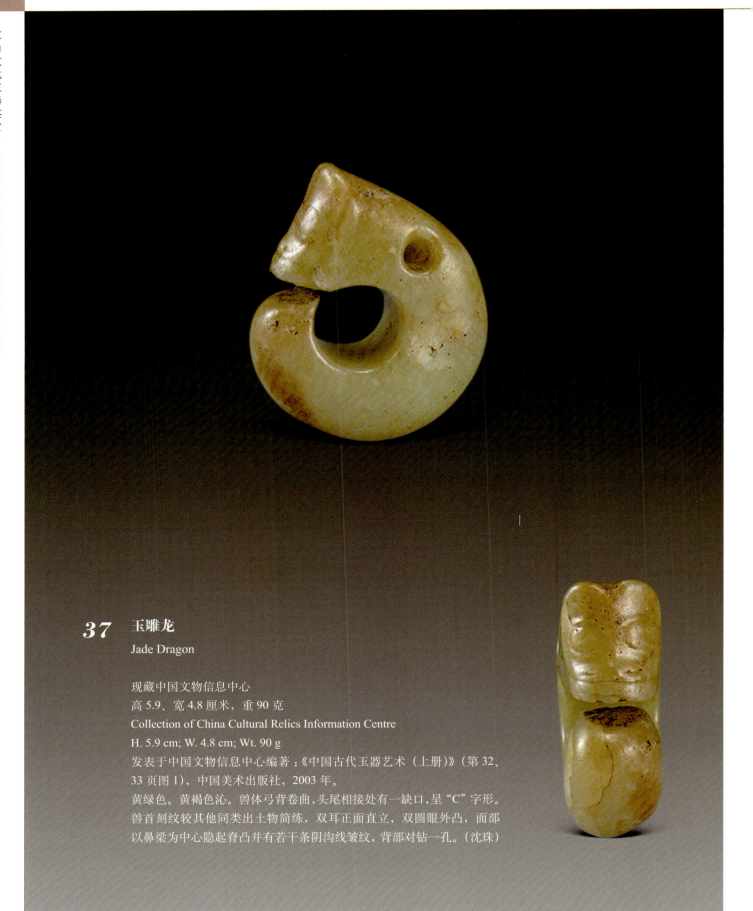

37 玉雕龙

Jade Dragon

现藏中国文物信息中心
高 5.9、宽 4.8 厘米，重 90 克
Collection of China Cultural Relics Information Centre
H. 5.9 cm; W. 4.8 cm; Wt. 90 g
发表于中国文物信息中心编著：《中国古代玉器艺术（上册）》（第 32、33 页图 1），中国美术出版社，2003 年。
黄绿色。黄褐色沁。兽体弓背卷曲，头尾相接处有一缺口，呈"C"字形。兽首刻纹较其他同类出土物简练，双耳正面直立，双圆眼外凸，面部以鼻梁为中心隐起脊凸并有若干条阴沟线皱纹，背部对钻一孔。（沈珠）

38 玉璧

Jade *Bi* Disc

现藏中国文物信息中心

长 8.3 厘米，重 6.6 克

Collection of China Cultural Relics Information Centre

L. 8.3 cm; Wt. 6.6 g

发表于中国文物信息中心编著：《中国古代玉器艺术（上册）》（第 42、
43 页图 1），中国美术出版社，2003 年。

黄玉，有黄褐色沁。整器浑圆厚重。内外边缘磨制成钝刃状。上部两
个穿孔并有凹槽，两面凹槽的位置不同，一面是两孔之间平行横槽，
另一面是两个平行向上的竖槽。凹槽的形成，可能是当时为穿系方便
打磨的，也可能是由于使用的绳系过于粗糙佩戴日久形成的。（沈珠）

39 双联玉璧

Two-ring Jade *Bi* Disc

现藏中国文物信息中心
长 6.5、宽 4.1 厘米，重 15 克
Collection of China Cultural Relics Information Centre
L. 6.5 cm; W. 4.1 cm; Wt. 15 g
发表于中国文物信息中心编著：《中国古代玉器艺术（上册）》（第 45 页，
图 9），中国美术出版社，2003 年。
青玉。浅褐色沁。两璧相连，边缘磨制成纯刃状，虽然器体较薄，上
部一孔仍双面对钻，两侧钻孔方向则有差别，一面由上向下，衔接处
形成台痕，制作工艺呈现较原始状态。（沈珠）

40 玉鸮

Jade Owl

早年从天津外贸工艺品公司征购
后调拨天津博物馆
现藏天津博物馆
高 5.7、宽 5.2 厘米
Purchased from Tianjin Foreign Trade and Handicraft Company
Collection of Tianjin Museum
H. 5.7 cm; W. 5.2 cm

发表于《中国玉器全集·1·原始社会》（图版一八），河北美术出版社，
1992 年。

由黄玉琢成，玉质纯润。为圆雕正视展翅立鸮。嘴作鹰钩形，隐
起双圆圈形目，耸肩。两翅浅阳线雕羽毛纹。浅浮雕双足，足下
部阴线刻斜方格纹。背面颈部有两对对钻孔，其一钻齚。此玉鸮
造型简约概括，刀法遒劲，属玉雕中的精致之作。其形制与内蒙
古巴林右旗出土黄玉鸮极似。（徐春苓）

41 勾云形玉器

Jade in the Shape of Hook and Cloud

早年发现于天津市外贸工艺品公司玉器库
后调拨天津博物馆
现藏天津博物馆
长 10.8、宽 9.5 厘米
Found in the jade storehouse of Tianjin Foreign Trade and Handicraft
Company
Collection of Tianjin Museum
L. 10.8 cm、W. 9.5 cm
发表于《中国玉器全集·1·原始社会》（图版一二），河北美术出版社，
1992 年。

青绿色玉质，局部有红褐色沁。片状雕，形似龟，中间镂空一卷
云形孔，尾和四足也琢成卷钩状。正、反两面均磨成凹槽式沟，
通体边缘磨成钝刃，顶端头部有两个先磨成凹槽再单面钻成的孔。
（徐春苓）

42　勾云形玉器

Jade in the Shape of Hook and Cloud

天津已故鉴藏家顾得威旧藏

1964 年顾氏后人捐献天津市文化局

现藏天津艺术博物馆

长 16.5、宽 5.4 厘米

Formerly collected by Gu Dewei

Donated to Tianjin Cultural Bureau by Xu family, 1964

Collection of Tianjin Art Museum

L. 16.5 cm; W. 5.4 cm

发表于《中国玉器全集·1·原始社会》（图版一四），河北美术出版社，1992 年。

玉质呈青绿色，有褐色沁。两端各有一鸟首，鸟身呈卷曲状，中间镂空一卷云形的孔，鸟尾相连，鸟嘴部尖长，尾身随形磨成沟槽，下端有并排的凸棱，上端单面钻一小孔。磨制技术粗朴原始，而韵味奇奥恢美。（徐春苓）

43 勾云形玉器

Jade in the Shape of Hook and Cloud

1943 年天津顾得威先生为鉴藏家徐世章购于
北京恩华斋古玩店
1954 年徐氏后人捐献于天津市文化局
后调拨天津市历史博物馆
1957 年转拨天津市艺术博物馆
现藏天津博物馆
长 9.8、宽 16 厘米
Purchased by Gu Dewei in Beijing, 1943
Donated to Tianjin Cultural Bureau by Xu
family, 1954
Collection of Tianjin Museum
L. 9.8 cm; W. 16 cm
发表于《中国玉器全集·1·原始社会》（图版
一三），河北美术出版社，1992 年。
葵黄色玉琢成。片雕，不规则长方形，若倒卧
的凤鸟。器边缘呈双面刃状，表面随器形磨出
宽凹槽，槽底刻单阴线。上端中部单面钻一孔。
造型飘逸，线条流畅、舒美。（徐春苓）

44

44 葫芦形玉兽

Jade Animal in the Shape of Double Gourd

天津市外贸工艺品公司唐山道库验扣
后拨交天津市艺术博物馆
现藏天津博物馆
高 4.4、宽 2.1 厘米
Acquired from Tianjin Foreign Trade and
Handicraft Company
Collection of Tianjin Museum
H. 4.4 cm; W. 2.1 cm
发表于《中国玉器全集·1·原始社会》（图版
一七），河北美术出版社，1992 年。
玉呈淡黄色，柔润洁净。圆雕葫芦形兽，圆
首，鼓腹，无四肢。头顶有两个小立耳，浅
浮雕圆形大眼，凸吻，阴线刻划眉鼻。器身
光素无纹。腹底部出一圆形凸尾。颈后部横
向对穿一孔，孔内有螺旋纹。此兽形体小巧，
造型夸张概括，形象奇特，稚气可爱，至今
未见同类器出土。从玉质、雕琢风格、手法
看应属红山文化玉器范畴。（徐春苓）

43

45 斜口筒形玉器

Hoof-shaped Jade

天津市文物公司于东北征集

1986 年售于天津市历史博物馆

现藏天津博物馆

通高 9.8、最大口径 7 厘米

Acquired in northeast China by Tianjin Antiquity Company

Purchased by Tianjin Museum of History, 1986

Collection of Tianjin Museum

H. 9.8 cm; Dia. (mouth, max) 7 cm

玉质呈黄绿色，有灰白色土沁。器呈马蹄状，上端稍撇为斜坡形，边缘成钝刃，口沿有磨痕，器表琢磨光润，下口略小，底端平齐，无孔。（徐春苓）

46 玉雕龙

Jade Dragon

中国外贸工艺品进出口公司天津分公司征集
天津市文化局检验出口文物商品时扣留
1976 年拨交天津市历史博物馆
现藏天津博物馆
高 14、宽 9.5 厘米
Acquired by China Foreign Trade and Handicraft Import & Export Company,
Tianjin Branch
Collection of Tianjin Museum
H. 14 cm; W. 9.5 cm
发表于《中国玉器全集·1·原始社会》(图版二六),河北美术出版社,1992 年。
器由青绿色玉雕成。背部有裂纹且凹进不平,为原玉料皮壳遗留。猪首龙身形,
首尾衔接处缺而不断,风格古朴浑厚,颇具神韵。背部对钻二个穿孔,这在
红山文化玉猪龙雕刻中比较少见。(徐春苓)

47

47　玉雕龙
Jade Dragon

天津市文化局在外贸工艺品公司验扣
后拨交天津市艺术博物馆
现藏天津博物馆
高 8.7、宽 6.4 厘米
Acquired by Tianjin Cultural Bureau
Collection of Tianjin Museum
H. 8.7 cm; W. 6.4 cm

发表于《中国玉器全集·1·原始社会》（图版二九），河北美术出版社，1992 年。
器由灰青色玉琢成，间杂黄褐色沁。身卷曲，口断开。兽首刻划简练，两只半圆形竖耳，阴线刻圆眼及鼻翼，鼻孔微凹，以两道阴线显示唇部。中间圆孔平滑规整，整体雕琢简洁拙朴。（徐春苓）

48　玉雕龙首
Jade Dragon Head

天津外贸部门辗转从东北地区收购
现藏天津博物馆
高 3.5、宽 4.5 厘米
Purchased by Tianjin foreign trade authorities in
northeast China
Collection of Tianjin Museum
H. 3.5 cm; W. 4.5 cm

发表于《中国玉器全集·1·原始社会》（图版三一），河北美术出版社，1992 年。
器由淡黄色玉琢成，肥首大耳，眼睛所在部位由对穿大孔代替，面部有阴刻线多道，吻部前伸，略向上翘，鼻端有二个窝状鼻孔，短颈，颈下有短榫。与红山文化的玉猪龙风格相似，应同属红山文化遗物。（徐春苓）

48

49 **玉雕龙**

Jade Dragon

北京米祥莆原藏
1954 年米氏欲出售给河北省博物馆未成交而后流入锦州市
1963 年天津市文物公司由锦州市文物商店购得
后售给天津艺术博物馆
现藏天津博物馆
高 14.1、宽 10.4 厘米
Formerly Collected by Mi Xiangpu
Unfulfilled sale to Hebei Provincial Museum by Mi family in 1954, later flown into
the market of Jinzhou, Liaoning
Purchased from Jinzhou Antiquity Shop by Tianjin Antiquity Company and later
sold to Tianjin Art Museum in 1963
Collection of Tianjin Museum
H. 14.1cm; W. (max) 10.4cm

发表于《文物天地》2009 年 6 期，徐春苓；《玉出红山脉 神游西辽河——天
津博物馆藏红山文化玉器巡礼》。

黄绿色，质地纯润。卷身，首尾相对，口断开，阴线刻兽首，两耳高耸，巨目圆睁，
双唇紧闭，鼻孔浅凹，鼻间及眼周有多道阴线饰纹，气势威武凶悍，神韵怪异。
余部雕刻极简，背脊对穿一孔，琢磨光润平匀，线条爽利流畅。圆雕与线刻
相结合是这件杰作的工艺特点，堪称红山文化玉器中的经典之作。（徐春苓）

50 "璋" 形玉器

Jade in the Shape of *Zhang* Tablet

由外省文物商店提供
现藏天津博物馆
高 12.5、宽 4.1 厘米
From an antiquity shop outside Tianjin
Collection of Tianjin Museum
H. 12.5cm; W. 4.1cm

发表于《文物天地》2009 年 6 期，徐春苓：《玉出红山脉 神游西辽河——天津博物馆藏红山文化玉器巡礼》。

青绿色，有少量黄褐色沁。器扁薄，轮廓若"丫"字形，两面纹饰相同。上部琢猪首，两耳直立外凸，阴线刻圆圈眼，凸雕扁宽形大嘴，体饰多道平行的凸弦纹。末端有一圆穿，可供穿系。类似器物在红山文化遗物中已发现多件，虽用途不甚明确，但其雕刻手法与玉猪龙有异曲同工之妙。（徐春苓）

51 勾云形玉珮

Celadonish Jade Pendant in the Shape of
Hook and Cloud

由外省文物商店提供
现藏天津博物馆
高 14.8、宽 6 厘米
From an antiquity shop outside Tianjin
Collection of Tian jin Museum
H. 14.8cm; W. 6cm
发表于《文物天地》2009 年 6 期，徐春苓：
《玉出红山脉 神游西辽河——天津博物馆
藏红山文化玉器巡礼》。
青玉，多土黄色沁。单面雕。正面略凸，
并随形刻粗阴线，线条遒劲。边缘薄锐，
尖端微勾卷，中部形制呈对角形对称。反
面中心位置磨有两道凹槽，槽底部对穿一
孔。造型奇妙，若一朵浮云。（徐春苓）

52

52 角形玉器

Horn-shaped Jade

天津市外贸工艺品公司验扣品
1990 年拨交天津市历史博物馆
现藏天津博物馆
高 11.6、宽 4.4 厘米
Acquired from Tianjin Foreign Trade and
Handicraft Company
Transferred to Tianjin Museum of History in
1990
Collection of Tianjin Museum
H. 11.6cm; W. 4.4cm
发表于《文物天地》2009 年 6 期，徐春苓：
《玉出红山脉 神游西辽河——天津博物馆藏
红山文化玉器巡礼》。
葵黄色，多黄褐色沁。玉兽角上端刻角棱纹，
下端呈弯钩状。类似觿。背面一侧边缘有一
纵向穿带孔。（徐春苓）

51

53　**双蛇首玉梳背饰**

Jade Comb Ornament with Two Snake Heads

天津已故鉴藏家顾得威旧藏
1954 年顾氏后人捐献天津市文化局
1957 年转拨天津市艺术博物馆
现藏天津博物馆
高 2.7、长 7 厘米
Formerly collected by Gu Dewei
Donated to Tianjin Cultural Bureau by Gu family, 1954
Collection of Tianjin Museum
H. 2.7 cm; L. 7 cm
发表于《文物天地》第 216 期（第 37 页），2009 年。
淡黄绿色玉质。体横长，并排三孔，与牛河梁遗址出土的双
兽首三孔玉梳背饰（见本书 58~59 页）相近，但此器两端饰
上昂的蛇首，最具特征。

54 玉鸮

Jade Owl

传世品
20 世纪 60 年代入藏上海博物馆
现藏上海博物馆
长 4.4、宽 4.4 厘米
Handed down
Collection of Shanghai Museum
L. 4.4 cm; W. 4.4 cm

玉质呈黄绿色，有杂斑。造型作扁平状，头部圆凸，两翼对称
平展，尾部平齐，全身光素无纹；器背面穿一对钻的牛鼻孔。
类似玉鸮在内蒙古巴林右旗、辽宁阜新胡头沟等红山文化考古
发掘中均曾有发现。（张尉）

55 玉蚕蛹

Jade Silkworm Pupa

上海文物商店旧藏
后由上海博物馆征集
现藏上海博物馆
高 5、宽 1.5 厘米
Formerly collected by Shanghai Antiquity Shop
Acquired by Shanghai Museum
Collection of Shanghai Museum
H. 5 cm; W. 1.5 cm

玉质呈黄色，间红褐色。圆雕成弯弧的蛹形，头部琢出凸眼，双耳，背部中脊分出两翼，腹部刻出皮纹，颈部穿一孔。这种玉蚕造型虽然在红山文化考古发掘中尚未得见，但从题材、琢工、玉质等各方面看，应归属红山文化。

我国是世界上最早发明丝绸的国家，历史上就有嫘祖始蚕的传说。东北地区素产柞蚕，柞蚕丝业也起源于我国。此蚕从形态、大小、色泽等方面与自然柞蚕皆颇相契合。蚕在古代具有多重的祥瑞含义，这种玉蚕应为当时红山先民崇奉的蚕神。（张尉）

美国
UNITED STATES

56 勾云形玉器

Jade in the Shape of Hook and Cloud

美国哈力（Erwin Harris）原藏
现藏华盛顿赛克勒博物馆
长 17.2 厘米
Formerly Collected by Erwin Harris
Collection of Arthur M. Sackler Gallery
L. 17.2 cm

发表于江伊莉《红山文化玉器与丰收祭仪》，Arts Asiatiques,1991 年；又
见苏芳淑《弗勒尔美术馆的一件红山文化玉饰》，Orientatilns,May,1993。
苏文中公布了原收藏者哈力先生 1945~1946 年有这件玉器的收藏品图片。
此器有明确的正、反面之分。短边的一侧略宽，另一侧略窄，并不对称。
长侧的一边齿突甚锐，另一长侧边则甚为平齐，疑有后期加工的原因。

6

57 **斜口筒形玉器**

（Ovel Tube , Possibly a Hair Ornament, 蹄形饰品

编号 B60J226）

Hoof-shaped Jade

来自辽宁

艾弗里 布朗帝奇（Avery Brundage 的音译）的藏品

现藏旧金山亚洲艺术馆藏

公元前 4700~2920 年

高 15.2 厘米

From Liaoning Province

Avery Brundage Collection

Collection of Asian Art Museum of San Francisco

4700 − 2920 BC

H. 15.2 cm

发表于达祥西 d'Argence：《步伦达治所藏的中国玉器》（图一八），1972 年。

软玉。位于中国东北部的红山文化制造的玉器与稍微偏南一点的良渚文化遗址出土的玉器在形态和装饰上稍有不同，这种类似马蹄形的物件在红山墓葬中被放置在死者头部或胳膊附近，应该是戴在头上的头扣或发簪。（旧金山亚洲艺术馆）

Here are some further remarks about the object by the curator:

"Located in northeast China, the Hongshan culture produced jades in shapesand decor slightly different from those found in Liangzhu culture sitesfurther south. Found in Hongshan burials and placed near the head or arm of the deceased, this type of object, shaped like a horse's hoof, is thoughtto have been worn asa hair clasp."　(Aion Tolme)

58 玉璧

Jade *Bi* Disc

芝加哥美术馆爱德华和路易斯·B·索南齐收
藏，1950·790
现藏芝加哥美术馆
公元前 3000 年
径 13.3×0.4 厘米

Art Institute of Chicago, the Edward and Louise
B. Sonnenschein Collection, 1950.790

Art Institute of Chicago

3000 BC

Dia.13.3 × 0.4 cm

发表于萨尔莫尼：《桑纳修所藏的中国古玉》
（图一〇三，三），1952 年。

玉质白而微透，有红褐色斑。内圆孔外方形。
无论玉料及造型、工艺，均为一件红山文化
典型器。（Elinor Pearlstein 潘思婷）

59 玉鸮

Jade Owl

塞利格曼遗赠 BM 1973.7~26.116,
现藏大英博物馆
公元前 3500 年
宽 5.2 厘米
BM 1973.7-26.116, Seligman bequest
Collection of the British Museum
3500 BC
W. 5.2 cm

发表于 JESSICA RAWSON：CHINESE JADE, Published for the Trustees of the British Museum by British Museum Press, 2005, P114；又见韩复思：《中国古代玉雕》，1968 年，图 1b，当时定为新石器时代（此书收有红山文化玉雕龙、勾云形玉器、斜口筒形玉器、玉鸟等，所定年代各有不同，唯将玉鸟定为新石器时代，在 20 世纪 80 年代初红山文化玉器研究成果公布前有此认识，难能可贵。编著者注）。

玉器不仅被用作仪式性的武器和工具，也被新石器时代的人们雕刻成装饰品和小动物。这件玉鸟是当时非常流行的典型的红山文化类型的玉器。在玉鸟伸展的翅膀上刻出脊和沟槽，这种纹饰在玉鸟三角形的尾部位置也重复出现。眼睛为突出的球状。在鸟的颈后部有穿孔。同样造型的器物在辽宁阜新胡头沟也有发现。

Jade was used not only to make ceremonial weapons and tools, but was also carved by some Neolithic peoples into ornaments and small animals. This bird is typical of the Hongshan culture type jades that were popular at that time. Its outstretched wings are incised with ridges or grooves which are also repeated on the triangular tail area. The eyes are prominently bulbous. There is a hole pierced through the back of his neck. Similar examples have been found at Hutougou in Fuxin, Liaoning province. （Carol Michaelson麦嘉乐）

60 斜口筒形玉器

Hoof-Shaped Jade

大英博物馆陈列何鸿卿藏玉器

现藏大英博物馆

公元前 3500 年

高 17、宽 11.5 厘米

Sir Joseph E. Hotung Collection of Jades

Collection of the British Museum

3500 BC

H. 17 cm; W. 11.5 cm

发表于 JESSICA RAWSON；CHINESE JADE，Published for the Trustees of the British Museum by British Museum Press，2005，P115。

此件器物形如一只伸展的、空心的马蹄。断面呈椭圆形，一端较平，沿底边向上逐渐变宽。一端受到侵蚀直至上端的开口，弯曲的一侧略高于较平的一侧。外侧较深的半圆形切割线形态的工具痕迹已经被认真磨光。在底部椭圆形断面的窄端有两个一侧钻的孔。玉器表面磨光。同样器物曾在红山文化墓葬中的死者头下发现，可能曾经作为束发器。

This hoof-shaped jade is shaped like an extended, hollow horse's hoof. Its section is oval, slightly flattened on one side and it widens from a fairly level lower edge, eroded on one side, to an even opening at the top, the curved side being slightly higher than the flattened one. Tool marks on the outside, in the form of deep semicircular cutting lines have been carefully smoothed. There are two holes at the bottom of the narrow points of the oval section, drilled from one side. The surface of the jade has a very soft matt polish. Similar pieces have been found beneath the heads of the dead in Hongshan graves and may once have had hair threaded through them? (Carol Michaelson 麦嘉乐)

61 　斜口筒形玉器

Hoof-Shaped Jade

大英博物馆陈列何鸿卿藏玉器

现藏大英博物馆

公元前 3500 年

高 4.6、宽 7.6 厘米

Sir Joseph E. Hotung Collection of Jades

Collection of the British Museum

3500 BC

H. (fragment) 4.6 cm; W. 7.6 cm

发表于 JESSICA RAWSON：CHINESE JADE, Published for the Trustees of the British Museum by British Museum Press, 2005，P116。

残，较 214 页介绍的玉器短。横断面为椭圆形，近似环状，一侧略高于另一侧，近似一个倒置的马蹄形，一角有损伤。在墓葬中发现的斜口筒形器多发现在墓主的头部，在某种程度上与头发有关。这类器物在红山文化墓葬中极为常见，几乎每座墓葬中都有一件，有些可见两件。

This is a shorter version of the above jade. It is oval in cross-section and consists of a ring, much taller on one side than the other, making an inverted hoof shape. One corner is damaged, where part of the flawed stone has fallen away. Most hoof-shaped jades found in graves have been found at the head of the tomb occupant and may have been attached to the hair in some way. They are common in Hongshan tombs, and although each tomb usually contains only one, occasionally there are two.（Carol Michaelson 麦嘉乐）

62 玉鸟

Jade Bird

大英博物馆陈列何鸿卿藏玉器

现藏大英博物馆

公元前 3500 年

高 4.2、宽 5.1 厘米

Sir Joseph E. Hotung Collection of Jades

Collection of the British Museum

3500 BC

H. 4.2 cm; W. 5.1 cm

发表于 JESSICA RAWSON ：CHINESE JADE，Published for the Trustees of the British Museum by British Museum Press，2005，P117。

鸟是红山文化坠饰的基本类型。此件玉鸟随着时间的流逝被磨成圆形，身体微弓，在小的扁平的头下有伸展的翅膀。突出的胸部略高于翅膀线，两个水平方向的沟纹将其与装饰有交叉线的三角形区域区分开来。翅膀上的纵向沟纹由于佩戴已被磨平，背部的切割线也几乎被磨平。隧孔略偏离中心位置。

Birds are one of the principal categories of Hongshan pendant. Worn over time into a rounded form, this bird has bowed, outstretched wings below a small flattened head. A raised breast protrudes slightly above the level of the wings, two horizontal grooves marking the division from the small triangular area decorated with cross-hatching. Vertical grooves on the wings have been smoothed down by wear, and on the back, uneven cutting is also completely smoothed down. A biconical hole is slightly off-centre.（Carol Michaelson 麦嘉乐）

63 玉雕龙

Jade Dragon

塞利格曼遗赠 1973.7~26.140,
现藏大英博物馆
公元前 3500 年
长 10.4 厘米
British Museum 1973.7-26.140, Seligman bequest
Collection of the British Museum
3500 BC
L. (fragment) 10.4 cm

发表于 JESSICA RAWSON：CHINESE JADE，Published for the Trustees of the British Museum by British Museum Press，2005，P116。

体下部残缺，仅残存上部。尽管我们能看到的只是整体造型的一部分，但这种动物应当是某种特定类型的猪龙形玉饰。在这些猪龙的脸部可以看到一种相当复杂的造型设计。器表和边缘切割沟纹可能是由某种旋转的切割工具（砣具）造成的，切割留下宽而浅的"V"字形沟纹。

This animal must have been a particularly imposing variety of pig-dragon ornament as we are only left with this fragment of it. A very sophisticated level of modelling is seen on the faces of these pig-dragons. Some sort of cutting tool, possibly a rotating one was used to cut grooves on the surface and at the corners of many pieces. These cutting lines left wide, fairly shallow v-shaped grooves. （Carol Michaelson 麦嘉乐）

64　玉雕龙

Jade Dragon

大英博物馆陈列品何鸿卿藏玉器

现藏大英博物馆

公元前 3500 年

高 6.3、宽 5 厘米

Sir Joseph E. Hotung Collection of Jades

Collection of the British Museum

3500 BC

H. 6.3 cm; W. 5 cm

发表于 JESSICA RAWSON：CHINESE JADE, Published for the Trustees of the British Museum by British Museum Press, 2005, P117。

这是一款较为典型的卷钩状猪龙，是红山文化玉器雕刻的主要类型。较厚的身体盘卷呈圆形，尖锥形尾部紧靠强有力的头部的平直的下颚。颈部卷曲不如尾部明显，形成非对称的形态。头部具有典型特征，有圆但不明显的尖角，突出的眼睛和鼻孔，在平的下颚上有细微磨线形成的唇部，构成身体的中心孔和颈部背面的悬挂孔都是双面钻的。在上侧的穿孔中研磨遗留的痕迹可以在小的同心线中发现。

This is a typical coiled pig-dragon, one of the principal types of Hongshan culture jade carving. Its thick body coils round so that the tapering, pointed tail abuts the straight jaw of the powerful head. The neck is less tightly turned than the tail, making for an asymmetrical profile. The head has the characteristic features of rounded but slightly pointed horns, bulging eyes and nostrils, and lips in faint moulded lines above the flattened jaw. Both the central hole which created the body and a suspension hole in the back of the neck have been drilled from both sides. In the upper hole traces of the abrading material can be seen in small concentric scored lines.（Carol Michaelson 麦嘉乐）

65 **玉雕龙**
Jade Dragons

吉斯拉原藏（Gieseler Collection）
现藏巴黎吉美美术馆
高 15.3 厘米
Formerly Giessler collection
Collection of Musée Guimet
H. 15.3 cm

发表于 Una Pope-Hennessy, Early Chinese Jades, Ernest Benn, Limeted
8 Bouverie Stree E.C.4, London, Plate ⅩⅩⅡ fig. 2(《早期中国玉器》
图版二二）；又见韩思复：《中国古代玉雕》（图五四）（定为公元前
3 世纪楚国风格），1968 年；邓淑苹：《谈谈红山系玉器》（第 74 页
图八），（台）《故宫文物月刊》189 卷，1998 年。

淡绿色，通体有大片红褐色瑕斑覆盖，质地硬，而刻线甚为均匀、
流畅，且在耳、目部线纹之间的打洼浅而规整清晰，是此类玉雕龙
中个体较大、工艺较精的一件。

7 资料部分
SUPPLEMENTS

1 ARCHAEOLOGICAL FINDINGS

1. Jade in the Shape of Hook and Cloud
2. Jade in the Shape of Hook and Cloud
3. Jade Bird

2 COLLECTIONS UNEARTHED FROM ARCHAEOLOGICAL POINTS (NOT AVAILABLE)

3 COLLECTIONS FROM ARCHAEOLOGICAL SITES

1. Stone Fish
2. Jade Axe

4 COLLECTIONS UNEARTHED FROM CERTAIN SITES

1. Jade Axe
2. Ring-shaped Jade

5 COLLECTIONS UNEARTHED FROM CERTAIN REGIONS

1. Jade in the Shape of Hook and Cloud
2. Jade in the Shape of Hook and Cloud

6 OTHER IMPORTANT COLLECTIONS

1. Jade Silkworm
2. Owl-shaped Celadonish Jade Pendant
3. Owl-shaped Celadonish Jade Pendant
4. Celadonish Jade Pendant in the Shape of Silkworm Pupa
5. Celadonish Jade Pendant in the Shape of Hook and Cloud
6. Celadonish Jade Pendant in the Shape of Hook and Cloud
7. 8. Jade *Bi* Disc
9. Jade Dragon
10. Jade Dragon
11. Coiled Jade Dragon
12. Hoof-shaped Jade
13. Hoof-shaped Jade
14. Hoof-shaped Jade
15. Hoof-shaped Jade
16. Hoof-shaped Jade
17. Hoof-shaped Jade
18. Hoof-shaped Jade
19. Hoof-shaped Jade
20. Hoof-shaped Jades
21. Jade in the Shape of Hook and Cloud
22. Jade in the Shape of Hook and Cloud
23. Jade in the Shape of Hook and Cloud
24. Jade Bird
25. Jade Bird
26. Jade Bird
27. Jade Human Figure
28. Jade Human Figure
29. Jade Human Figure
30. Jade Arm Ornament
31. Hoof-shaped Jade
32. Bird-shaped Jade

1　考古发掘品

1. 勾云形玉器

2. 勾云形玉器

3. 玉鸟

2　有出土单位的收集品（缺）

3　遗址收集品

1. 石鱼

2. 玉斧

4　有出土地点的收集品

1. 玉斧

2. 玉环

5　有出土地区的收集品

1. 勾云形玉器

2. 勾云形玉器

6　其他珍贵收集品

1. 玉蚕蛹

2. 鸮形玉珮

3. 鸮形玉珮

4. 蚕蛹形玉珮

5. 勾云形玉珮

6. 勾云形玉珮

7. 8. 玉璧

9. 玉雕龙

10. 玉雕龙

11. 附脊玉雕龙

12. 斜口筒形玉器

13. 斜口筒形玉器

14. 斜口筒形玉器

15. 斜口筒形玉器

16. 斜口筒形玉器

17. 斜口筒形玉器

18. 斜口筒形玉器

19. 斜口筒形玉器

20. 斜口筒形玉器

21. 勾云形玉器

22. 勾云形玉器

23. 勾云形玉器

24. 玉鸟

25. 玉鸟

26. 玉鸟

27. 玉人

28. 玉人

29. 玉人

30. 玉臂饰

31. 斜口筒形玉器

32. 鸟形玉器

1 考古发掘品
ARCHAEOLOGICAL FINDINGS

1.勾云形玉器（大甸子墓821:5，镂花雕）

内蒙古敖汉旗大甸子夏家店下层文化墓葬出土。现藏中国社会科学院考古研究所。线图与图版分别发表于中国社会科学院考古研究所：《大甸子——夏家店下层文化遗址与墓地发掘报告》（第 174 页图八三，15；图版五二，3），科学出版社，1998 年。

高 3.3、宽 6.9、厚 0.4 厘米。淡绿色。形小。单钩形，体面瓦沟纹较深。长边一侧起凸近于双钩形勾云形玉器的齿状凸，是单钩形勾云形玉器与双钩形勾云形玉器为同类的明证。所出位置在胸部也同于红山文化，可见传承之紧密。

Jade in the Shape of Hook and Cloud

Unearthed from Lower Xiajiadian Culture tomb at Dadianzi, Aohan,

Inner Mongolia Autonomous Region

Collection of Institute of Archaeology, Chinese Academy of Social Sciences

H. 3.3 cm; W. 6.9 cm; T. 0.4 cm

2.勾云形玉器（琉璃河燕国墓 M1029：24）

1981~1983 年北京琉璃河西周燕国墓地第 1029 号墓出土。发表于《考古》1984 年第 5 期，中国社会科学院考古研究所、北京市文物工作队琉璃河考古队：《1981~1983 年琉璃河西周燕国墓地发掘简报》〔第 415 页图一二，7；图版肆（一），8〕。

长 5.5 厘米。一半残缺。青绿色。镂空雕，除长边一侧正中有钻孔外，近残边处及中心卷钩处也有钻孔。红山文化玉器以残件出现的，以勾云形玉器为最多，在红山文化墓葬中，就有以勾云形玉器残件随葬的实例，此残件应为红山文化流传到西周燕国时期的，也可见红山文化玉器流传时间之长。

Jade in the Shape of Hook and Cloud

Unearthed from Western Zhou Tomb 1029 of Yan State at Liulihe,

Beijing, 1981 — 1983

L. (fragment) 5.5 cm

3. 玉鸟（虢国墓地 编号 M2001 ： 669-11）

河南三门峡西周晚期虢国墓地出土。现藏河南省文物考古研究所。又称鹰
形佩，见秦曙光、姜涛:《虢国墓出土玉器概况及所出红山玉器》，（台）《海
峡两岸古玉学会议论文专辑（1）》，2001 年。
长宽均为 5.3、最厚处 1.4 厘米。出土时位于墓主人脑后，为一组呈 "T"
字形组合发饰中的一件。青玉，大部分受沁呈灰白色。玉质细腻微透明。
圆雕，鸟背上鼓，中部与尾部各有一个透穿圆孔。尾部穿孔较细，为单面
钻，胸部平坦，有一对穿象鼻孔。

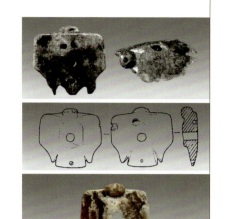

Jade Bird

Unearthed from late Western Zhou tomb of Guo State at Sanmenxia, Henan
Province

Collection of Henan Provincial Institute of Cultural Relics and Archaeology

L. 5.3 cm; W. 5.3 cm; T. (max) 1.4 cm

2 有出土单位的收集品（缺）
COLLECTIONS UNEARTHED FROM ARCHAEOLOGICAL POINTS (NOT AVA ILABLE)

3 遗址收集品
COLLECTIONS FROM ARCHAEOLOGICAL SITES

1.石鱼

内蒙古赤峰巴林右旗巴彦汉苏木那日斯台遗址出土。20 世纪 80 年代初巴
林右旗博物馆征集。现藏巴林右旗博物馆。发表于《考古》1987 年 6 期，
巴林右旗博物馆：《内蒙巴林右旗那斯台遗址调查》（线图见第 517 页图
一五，6）。长 4.3 厘米。翠绿色石。扁圆锥形，头颈部有一周阴刻弦纹，
似为鱼腮，双目对透呈孔，凹坑式圆嘴，左侧顺体刻一条沟痕，右侧似为
两条鱼翅，尾端变细呈尖尾。琢磨不够规整。

Stone Fish

Unearthed at Bairin Right Banner, Chifeng, Inner Mongolia Autonomous Region

Collection of Bairin Right Banner Museum

L. 4.3 cm

2.玉斧

内蒙古敖汉旗牛古吐乡千斤营子遗址出土。现藏敖汉旗博物馆。发表于邵国田主编：《敖汉文物精华》（第 73 页），内蒙古文化出版社，2004 年。
长 25、刃宽 7.1、顶端宽 4 厘米。墨玉，质细腻，有灰白相间的条状纹理，微有透明。通体磨光，两侧边有外弧，顶端扁平且有粗糙面，弧刃向一侧倾斜。近刃口的两面有斜向使用痕迹。

Jade Axe

Unearthed at Qianjinyingzi site, Aohan, Inner Mongolia Autonomous Region

Collection of Aohan Banner Museum

L. 25 cm; W. (blade) 7.1 cm, (top) 4 cm

4 有出土地点的收集品
COLLECTIONS UNEARTHED FROM CERTAIN SITES

1.玉斧

内蒙古敖汉旗长胜镇北泡子沿村出土。现藏于敖汉旗博物馆。发表于邵国田主编：《敖汉文物精华》（第 73 页），内蒙古文化出版社，2004 年。
长 19、宽 7 厘米。浅绿色，质细腻。体散布黄、白色斑。通体磨光，体扁平，两侧边稍有外弧，刃部圆弧，近刃部两面有使用痕迹。

Jade Axe

Unearthed at Beipaoziyan, Aohan, Inner Mongolia Autonomous Region

Collection of Aohan Banner Museum

L. 19 cm; W. 7 cm

2.玉环

河北省围场县下伙房收集。原藏围场县博物馆。外径 11.3、内径 6、厚 5.3 厘米。环体近于正圆形，甚为肥厚，内孔缘磨平而不起棱脊。类似器见于牛河梁遗址"采标本 8"〔见辽宁省文物考古研究所编著：《牛河梁—红山文化遗址发掘报告》（1983~2003 年度）中册 466 页图一一，1；下册图版三一八，2，文物出版社，2012 年〕。

Ring-shaped Jade

Collected at Xiahuofang, Weichang, Hebei Province

Collection of Weichang Museum

Dia. (outer) 11.3cm; Dia. (inner) 6cm; T. 5.3cm

5 有出土地区的收集品
COLLECTIONS UNEARTHED FROM CERTAIN REGIONS

1.勾云形玉器

内蒙古阿鲁科尔沁旗征集。现藏赤峰市博物馆。发表于张乃仁等著：《辽海奇观——辽河流域的古代文明》（第35页），天津人民出版社，1989年。长12.9、宽9.5厘米。青灰玉。为单钩形。体较宽，近于方形。四角卷钩富于变化，器面磨出随器形变化走向的瓦沟纹。长边一侧正中钻单孔。

Jade in the Shape of Hook and Cloud

Acquired at Ar Horqin, Chifeng, Inner Mongolia Autonomous Region

Collection of Chifeng Antiquity Shop

L. 12.9 cm; W. 9.5 cm

2. 勾云形玉器

内蒙古阿鲁科尔沁旗收集。发表于《文物》1984年6期，孙守道、郭大顺：《论辽河流域的原始文明与龙的起源》（第14页图五）。长15.2、宽10.7、厚0.45厘米。淡绿色。方圆形，短边一侧两角的两卷钩方向相同，长边一端中部有对称双钻孔。体面磨出随器体变化走向的瓦沟纹。

Jade in the Shape of Hook and Cloud

Collected at Ar Horqin, Chifeng, Inner Mongolia Autonomous Region

L. 15.2 cm; W. 10.7 cm; T. 0.45 cm

6 其他珍贵收集品
OTHER IMPORTANT COLLECTIONS

1.玉蚕蛹

现藏中国文物信息中心。发表于中国文物信息中心编著：《中国古代玉器艺术（上册）》（第74、75页图23），中国美术出版社，2003年。高1.5、长1.4、宽1.7厘米，重27克。黄绿色玉，平顶，尾端圆弧，两侧及腹部为弯凹状，首端的平面上以双圈纹作蛹目，背部以数道凸弦纹饰作简化的躯体，腰部有一对穿孔，应为佩饰。蛹体纹饰简练，身体肥壮。（田苏萍）

Jade Silkworm

Collection of China Cultural Relics Information Centre

H. 1.5 cm; L. 1.7 cm; W. 1.4 cm; Wt. 27 g

2.鸮形玉珮

早年从天津外贸工艺品公司征购，后拨交天津博物馆。现藏天津博物馆。
发表于《文物天地》2009 年 6 期，徐春苓：《玉出红山脉 神游西辽河——天津博物馆藏红山文化玉器巡礼》。
高 4.8、宽 4.6 厘米。青白玉，通身有浅黄色沁。鹰首作三角形，弯至胸部。双翅横展，并用阳刻线表示羽毛，若隐若现。右翅膀下部有穿孔。爪部用一道阳线表示。背面靠颈部位置有一对斜穿孔，可供穿系。

Owl-shaped Celadonish Jade Pendant

Acquired from Tianjin Foreign Trade and Handicraft Company

Transferred to Tianjin Museum

Collection of Tianjin Museum

H. 4.8cm; W. 4.6cm

3. 鸮形玉珮

由外省文物商店提供。现藏天津博物馆。发表于《文物天地》2009 年 6 期，徐春苓：《玉出红山脉 神游西辽河——天津博物馆藏红山文化玉器巡礼》。
高 5.5、宽 5.1 厘米。淡绿色，呈正立展翅静待状。阴线刻圆圈眼，以阳线饰羽纹。反面颈部一纵向对穿孔。雕琢简练概括。

Owl-shaped Celadonish Jade Pendant

From an antiquity shop outside Tianjin

Collection of Tianjin Museum

H. 5.5cm; W. 5.1cm

4. 蚕蛹形玉珮

天津市外贸工艺品公司验扣品，后拨交天津博物馆。现藏天津博物馆。发表于《文物天地》2009 年 6 期，徐春苓：《玉出红山脉 神游西辽河——天津博物馆藏红山文化玉器巡礼》。
长 5.9、宽 3.1 厘米。黄玉质，形体较厚。蚕首端较平，尾端圆尖，背凹弯。首端以圆圈纹作双目，背部以五道凸弦纹作身躯。首端至尾端通体穿孔，与腰间的横穿相通，孔内有螺旋纹。造型与内蒙古巴林右旗出土的玉蚕相似，只惜背部后刻两道深凹槽，但并不妨碍对其原貌的识别。

Celadonish Jade Pendant in the Shape of Silkworm Pupa

Acquired from Tianjin Foreign Trade and Handicraft Company

Transferred to Tianjin Museum

Collection of Tianjin Museum

L. 5.9cm; W. 3.1cm

5. 勾云形玉珮

由外省文物商店提供。现藏天津博物馆。发表于《文物天地》2009 年 6 期，徐春苓：《玉出红山脉 神游西辽河——天津博物馆藏红山文化玉器巡礼》。长 10.5、宽 7.1 厘米。青绿色，多白色沁。器体扁薄，呈长方形，中心部位镂空，作一勾云状卷角。通体磨宽浅凹槽，两侧各外伸一对钩角，上端对穿两个圆孔。

Celadonish Jade Pendant in the Shape of Hook and Cloud

From an antiquity shop outside Tianjin

Collection of Tianjin Museum

L. 10.5cm; W. 7.1cm

6. 勾云形玉珮

由外省文物商店提供。现藏天津博物馆。发表于《文物天地》2009 年 6 期，徐春苓《玉出红山脉 神游西辽河——天津博物馆藏红山文化玉器巡礼》。高 3.6、残长 7.5 厘米。淡绿色。单面片雕，虽残缺，但不失红山文化勾云形玉珮之风格。底出四齿，一齿残断。

Celadonish Jade Pendant in the Shape of Hook and Cloud

From an antiquity shop outside Tianjin

Collection of Tianjin Museum

H. 3.6cm; L. (fragment) 7.5cm

7.8. 玉璧

由外省文物商店提供。现藏天津博物馆。发表于《文物天地》2009 年 6 期，徐春苓：《玉出红山脉 神游西辽河——天津博物馆藏红山文化玉器巡礼》。一环直径 7.4 厘米，另一环直径 7.1 厘米。似为一对，大小略异。青白玉，有浅黄色沁。器呈不规整圆形，做工古朴，孔缘留有系挂痕迹。此对玉环与牛河梁等地红山文化石棺墓所出玉环近似。

Jade *Bi* Disc

From an antiquity shop outside Tianjin

Collection of Tianjin Museum

Dia. 7.4cm

Dia. 7.1cm

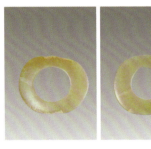

9. 玉雕龙

现藏上海博物馆。发表于上海市文物管理委员会编：《鉴余留珍》（第 197 页图 5），上海古籍出版社，2008 年。

长 6.8、宽 5.8 厘米。红褐色，体卷曲如环，头部较小，双耳竖立较高，吻前突。

Jade Dragon

Collection of Shanghai Museum

L. 6.8 cm; W. 5.8 cm

10. 玉雕龙

天津武清区十四仓清代墓葬出土。现藏天津市文化遗产保护中心。发表于《中国出土玉器全集·1》（第 103 页），科学出版社，2005 年。

高 10.4、宽 8.4、厚 4.0 厘米。白色泛灰，有浅黑色瑕斑。耳较厚，五官位置较为紧凑。为红山文化遗物。在时代晚于红山文化的遗存中出土的红山文化玉器，前期如先秦时期与后期如出土这件标本的清代，其含义应有所不同，前者具更多文化传承意义，而后者则可能与收藏鉴赏有关。

Jade Dragon

Unearthed from Qing tomb at Shisicang, Tianjin

Collection of Tianjin Cultural Heritage Protection Centre

H. 10.4 cm; W. 8.4 cm; T. 4 cm

11. 附脊玉雕龙

发表于傅忠谟著（傅熹年整理）：《古玉精英》（第 20~21 页图 5），（台北）中华书局有限公司，1989 年。

直径 28.2、曲长 42.2 厘米，重 502 克。绿玉。造型同于赛沁塔拉龙，唯体较粗。吻端面圆弧，吻部上卷甚为明显。且吻端起尖。

Coiled Jade Dragon

Dia. 28.2 cm; L. (curve) 42.2 cm; Wt. 502 g

12. 斜口筒形玉器 (Hair Tubes)

巴尔（A.W.Bahr.Bahr）收藏。发表于 Stanley Charles Nott: Chinese Jade Throughout the Ages（斯坦利 查理斯 诺特：《各时代的中国玉器》）（图版 xv 下），1936 年。又称发箍。巴尔氏曾于 1911 年出版 Jan Stuart Bahr, A. W. OLD CHINESE PORCELAIN AND WORK OF ART IN CHINA（《中国古代瓷器及中国艺术品》），伦敦，1911 年，该书是巴尔氏于 1908 年在上海所开的美术展览会（英国皇家亚细亚学会华北分会发起）3000 件陈列品中选编，共 120 幅，此件玉器是否展出，待考。

高 9.5 厘米。

Hoof-shaped Jade

Collection of A. W. Bahr

H. 9.5 cm

13. 斜口筒形玉器 (Headdress Ornament？)

现藏美国布法罗（水牛城）博物馆。发表于 Joan M Hartman.Anctent Chinese Jades from the Buffalo Museum of Science（《布法罗科学博物馆的中国古代玉器》），PI 81, 1975。

高 11.4 厘米。

Hoof-shaped Jade

Collection of Buffalo Museum of Science

H. 11.4 cm

14. 斜口筒形玉器 (Oval Tube)

现藏美国印第安那州明尼安那波利斯美术馆，编号 50．46．305。发表于 Harold Peterson , Chinse Jades fron the Minneapolis Institute of Arts , 1977 ; Introduction by Na Chih-liang in 1973（那志良、比得生：《明尼安那波利斯美术馆藏中国古代与近代玉器》，图九七，1977 年），定为周代。转引自（台）《故宫文物月刊》189 卷，邓淑苹：《谈谈红山系玉器》（第 73 页），1998 年。高 14.9 厘米。从照片看，体较窄，两端的宽度差别较小。

Hoof-shaped Jade
Collection of Minneapolis Institute of Arts
H. 14.9 cm

15.斜口筒形玉器

1950 年卢芹斋在美国佛罗里达州展出品，定为周代。发表于 C T Loo, Chinese Archaic Jades, 1950, PI XXXV Ⅱ（卢芹斋：《中国古玉》，图三七，三，1950 年）；图片转引自（台）《故宫文物月刊》189 卷，邓淑苹：《谈谈红山系玉器》（第 72 页图一），1998 年。
高 14.5 厘米。

Hoof-shaped Jade
H. 14.5 cm

16. 斜口筒形玉器

1969 年韩思复 (Howard Hansford) 为南非德裔收藏家欧兹 (Klaus D.Baron vonoertzen) 撰写的藏品图录。发表于 Howard Hansford, Jade, Essence of Hills and Streams. the Von Oertzen Collection of Chinese and Indian Jades. London. 1969（韩思复：《精神见于山川》，图七五，1969 年），定为汉代。转引于（台）《故宫文物月刊》189 卷，邓淑苹：《谈谈红山系玉器》（第 72 页），1998 年。
高 9.5 厘米。从照片看，斜口与平口的边缘都有内凹，这是制作时有意而为（即仿龟壳）还是使用时的磨损，有待进一步观察。

Hoof-shaped Jade
H. 9.5 cm

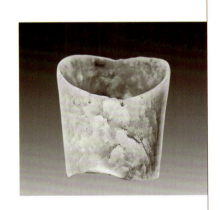

17. 斜口筒形玉器

现藏哈佛大学福格博物馆。发表于 Max Loehr, Ancient Chinese Jades from Grenville L Winthrop Collection, 1975m PI 324（罗越：《中国古玉——福格博物馆温索普收藏》，图三二四，1975 年），定为周代；转引自（台）《故宫文物月刊》189 卷，邓淑苹：《谈谈红山系玉器》（第 72 页图二），1998 年。高 18.9 厘米，淡绿色，间有白色斑点。为此类斜口筒形玉器中较大的一件，体长而甚宽，壁也较厚。尤其是短面的斜口一端有垂鳞纹，为五道弧线组成。垂鳞纹为红山文化吸收仰韶文化彩陶技法后创造的具有本文化特色即龙鳞纹的图案，此种图案在红山文化玉器上出现，是将红山文化彩陶与玉器相联系的又一例证。

Hoof-shaped Jade

Collection of Fogg Museum

H. 18.9 cm

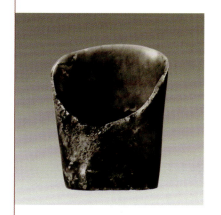

18.斜口筒形玉器(Ceremonial Cuff ?)

现藏美国哈佛大学福格博物馆。发表于 Max Loehr, Ancient Chinese Jades from Grenville L Winthrop Collection, 1975m PI 323（罗越：《中国古玉——福格博物馆温索普收藏》,图三二三,1975 年),转引自（台）《故宫文物月刊》189 卷，邓淑苹：《谈谈红山系玉器》（第 72 页），1998 年。

高 11.3 厘米。通体较短，短边一侧尤短，形成大斜口。

Hoof-shaped Jade

Collection of Fogg Museum

H. 11.3 cm

19. 斜口筒形玉器

罗越（Max Loehr）收藏。发表于 CHINESE ARCHAIC JADES AND BRONZES From the estate of Professor Max Loehr and others，1993（《罗越教授等人的玉器与铜器》，1993 年），内有罗越于 1944 年手绘图（右）。图片转引自（台）《故宫文物月刊》189 卷,邓淑苹:《谈谈红山系玉器》（第 72 页图三），1998 年。

高 12.9 厘米。

Hoof-shaped Jade

Collection of Max Loehr

H. 12.9 cm

20. 斜口筒形玉器

现藏沙可乐家族。发表于 Thomas Lawton, Asian Art in the Arthur M Sackler Galley. Jade section (《沙可乐艺术馆的亚洲艺术·玉器部分》), 1987, PI 32。
2 件, 分别高 14.6、15.8, 宽 9.5、9.7 厘米。

Hoof-shaped Jades

Collection of Sackler family

H. 14.6 cm; W. 9.5 cm

H. 15.8 cm; W. 9.7 cm

21.勾云形玉器(Toothed Pendants)

1938 年萨尔莫尼公布, 后经包尔由美国沙可乐收藏。发表于 Alfred Salmony, Carved Jade of Ancient China, 1938, PI V II .6（萨尔莫尼：《中国古代的玉雕》, 图七, 六, 1938 年), 称有齿坠饰。图版转引自（台）《故宫文物月刊》189 卷, 邓淑苹:《谈谈红山系玉器》(第 73 页图四), 1998 年。长 4.8 厘米。简化型。长边一侧起三齿凸, 长边另侧外弧, 正中近边一孔已残, 旁侧又钻一孔。

Jade in the Shape of Hook and Cloud

Collection of Sackler family

L. 4.8 cm

22. 勾云形玉器

1994 年佳士得公司拍卖品。发表于 Important Chinese Works of Art from The Arthur M. Sackler Collections, Christie's, New York, Dec. 1, 1994 (《佳士得公司 1994 年在纽约拍卖图录》, 图七五), 图版转引自（台）《故宫文物月刊》189 卷, 邓淑苹：《谈谈红山系玉器》(第 73 页图五), 1998 年。残长 8.9 厘米。为双钩形勾云形玉器的残器, 保留长边一侧卷钩及三齿凸、中心双卷钩。器上遗有朱砂。推测为遗于商周墓中的红山文化玉器。

Jade in the Shape of Hook and Cloud

Auctioned at Christie's, 1994

L. (fragment) 8.9 cm

23. 勾云形玉器

欧兹 (Klaus D.Baron von Oertzen) 收藏。发表于 Howard Hansford, Jade, Essence of Hills and Streams. the Von Oertzen Collection of Chinese and Indian Jades. London. 1969（韩思复：《精神见于山川》，1969 年），定为唐代以后；图版转引自（台）《故宫文物月刊》189 卷，邓淑苹：《谈谈红山系玉器》（第 74 页图七），1998 年。

长 9.5 厘米。近于方形。四角及中心卷钩明确。中心镂空部分甚为宽大。从图片看，器体打洼较深而窄，旁随以阴线，也较有特点。

Jade in the Shape of Hook and Cloud

Collection of Klaus D. Baron von Oertzen

L. 9.5 cm

24.玉鸟(Bird Pendant 915·7·53)

加拿大安大略皇家博物馆收藏。发表于 Doris Dohrenwend, Chinese Jades in the Royal Ontario Museum 1971, P43（多瑞文：《皇家安大略博物馆的中国玉器》，第 43 页，1971 年），定为西周。转引自（台）《故宫文物月刊》189 卷，邓淑苹：《谈谈红山系玉器》（第 75 页图一一），1998 年。

宽 5.9 厘米。背有横钻的单隧孔。

Jade Bird

Collection of Royal Ontario Museum

W. 5.9 cm

25. 玉鸟

现藏美国布法罗（水牛城）博物馆。发表于 Joan M Hartman , Ancient Chinese Jades from the Buffalo Museum of Science, 1975, PI 26。原定名为"蝉"(Cicada)，时代定为商或西周。

高 4 .5 厘米。墨玉质，翅尾内收甚，背面有横钻的一隧孔。

Jade Bird

Collection of Buffalo Museum of Science

H. 4.5 cm

26. 玉鸟

沙可乐 1980 年前收藏，1994 年佳士得公司拍卖。发表于 Important Chinese Works of Art from The Arthur M. Sackler Collections, Christie's, New York, Dec. 1, 1994（《佳士得公司 1994 年在纽约拍卖图录》，图八三），图版转引自（台）《故宫文物月刊》189 卷，邓淑苹：《谈谈红山系玉器》（第 75 页图一二），1998 年。

有甚短而圆的立耳，应为鸮类。翅与尾面光素，均无羽毛的表现。腹下有突起的横带，也见于阜新福兴地所出玉鸮。背面甚平，有横钻的一隧孔，位置紧靠头顶。

Jade Bird

Collection of Sackler family prior to 1980

Auctioned at Christie's, 1994

27. 玉人

现藏英国剑桥大学飞兹威廉博物馆。发表于 S Howard Hansford, Chinese Carved Jades, 1968, PI 59（韩思复：《中国古代玉雕》，图五九，1968 年），定为公元前 3 世纪（战国）楚国风格；馆内部资料定为危地马拉和洪都拉斯地区的玛雅文化。图版及描述转引或参考自（台）《故宫文物月刊》189 卷，邓淑苹：《谈谈红山系玉器》（第 76 页图一五），1998 年；又见徐琳：《三尊"红山玉人"像解析》，中国社会科学报，2010 年 2 月 2 日，博物版。

高 12.2 厘米。黄绿色，温润光泽，有褐色斑痕。人物坐像，蹲踞式。裸身。双手按于膝头。三角形脸，尖下颌，以浅浮雕表现五官，弯眉，菱形长眼，三角形鼻，小嘴。双手轻按于双膝，无脚，小腿下方踏一弯月形台形物。前胸未特别表现性征，但是两腿之间以极浅的浮雕凹纹显不规则的洞，表现女性性征。头顶上带一"高冠"。这一"高冠"，其实是前肢向上举起、头向上仰的"熊"。熊的两腋旁有似乳房般的凸起。背部可见熊冠向下延展到腰际，应为一个头戴用熊皮做成帽子和披风的女神或女巫，也可能表达红山居民信奉的人与熊的合体神。

这类玉人多为倚坐式，姿态与东山嘴遗址出土的陶塑孕妇雕像相同，臀下应另有依托物，也是将其归为红山文化的依据之一。

Jade Human Figure

Collection of Fitzwilliam Museum

H. 12.2 cm

28.玉人

现藏克里夫兰艺术博物馆。发表于 Alfred Salmony,Chinese Jade through the Wei Dynasty,1963（萨尔莫尼:《直到魏代的中国玉器》,图三五:四,1963 年）定为汉代。图版及描述转引自（台）《故宫文物月刊》189 卷，邓淑苹:《谈谈红山系玉器》（第 77 页图一六），1998 年。

高 11.2 厘米。体形也为蹲踞式，双手按于膝头，足底蹬半月形物。兽面似牛，有凸额与上翘的口吻，两个大尖耳与两对共四个尖端秃钝向上翘起的长角。有以为是人头上戴兽形帽的形象。

Jade Human Figure

Collection of Cleveland Museum of Art

H. 11.2 cm

29.玉人

现藏瑞典远东博物馆。发表于 Alfred Salmony,Chinese Jade through the Wei Dynasty，1963（萨尔莫尼:《直到魏代的中国玉器》图三五，五，1963 年），定为汉代，又见远东博物馆:《瑞典国家的伊瑞生收藏》图二，1989 年。图版及描述转引自（台）《故宫文物月刊》189 卷，邓淑苹:《谈谈红山系玉器》（第 76 页图一七），1998 年。

高 10.5 厘米。形与上件相近，唯脸部模糊，缺一耳与一角，也没有腿上弯月形物。

Jade Human Figure

Collection of Museum of Far Eastern Antiquities

H. 10.5 cm

30.玉臂饰（Arched Plaque，1943.50.626）

现藏哈佛大学艺术博物馆。发表于 Max Loehr:Ancient Chinese Jades from Grenville L Winthrop Colleection （《温索普收藏品中的中国古代玉器》），1975,PI371.

长 9.7 厘米。从图片上所见为弯板状，正面饰减地阳纹式的回字形瓦沟纹，饰纹均匀，简洁，光泽度强。

Jade Arm Ornament

Collection of Harvard Art Museum

L. 9.7 cm

31. 斜口筒形玉器

现藏大英博物馆。

体较短，斜面满雕饕餮纹，应为商代时加刻。

Hoof-shaped Jade

Collection of the British Museum

32.鸟形玉器

现藏旧金山亚洲艺术博物馆。发表于 d'Argence, Ren'e-Yvon Lefebvre, Chinese Jades in the Avery Brundage Collection(《布伦达治收藏的中国古玉》), The de Young Museum, San Francisco,1972.

长 7.9、宽 5 厘米。此形鸟为圆雕作品，光素无纹，手法概略，具红山文化玉器特点，但尚无出土实例。

Bird-shaped Jade

Collection of Asian Art Museum of San Francisco

L. 7.9 cm; H. 5 cm

附录：玉器鉴定的基本方法

◎ 洪殿旭

中国古代玉器的鉴定，除了掌握历史上各个时期玉器的地域范围，玉器的类型等基本特点之外，还要多读一些记载出土玉器的考古报告，选择知名度较高的博物馆、考古所等文博单位正式出版的玉器图录在手以供随时翻阅，并且还要经常到收藏有这一时期玉器的博物馆观察实物，对出土玉器的形制、造形、纹饰、雕工等细部特征熟记于心。如果有条件和机会能够经常上手观摩到经过正式考古或专家认可的馆藏玉器，则是增强感性认识的最佳途径。更重要的是，在前人以及当代被普遍认可的专家的经验基础之上，掌握一套适合自己的科学、实际的古代玉器鉴定的基本方法。

首先，要熟悉新石器时代各个考古学文化以及历史上各个时期玉器的材质特征，对常用玉材的质地、颜色、硬度、透明度、光泽以及其他物理特性要准确理解和掌握。如红山文化玉器的选材，主要是岫岩一带的闪石玉，包括"老玉"和"河磨玉"。

"老玉"包括原生矿和次生矿两种。原生矿是指产于辽宁省岫岩县细玉沟山顶原生矿采掘出来的闪石玉料。之所以称"老"，是由于山头有古代采玉矿坑，表明其开采时代久远，也有别于人们通常所说的岫岩蛇纹石玉，主要产于瓦沟。

"河磨玉"是老玉的一种，即其次生矿的一个品种。是指细玉沟谷两侧凹地中或细玉沟沟口东侧的白沙河河谷底部及两岸一级阶地的泥沙砾石层中的闪石玉砾石。亿万年前，细玉沟头山顶的原生玉石矿裸露于地表经过风化后成为大小不同的块状玉矿石，被山洪冲下山后，在河水里与各种滚漕河中的岩石一起滚动磨擦，日久天长便磨成没有棱角的砾石，因而被称为河磨玉。玉体表面经土浸、风化等原因形成石状包裹物，表面看恰似普通的石头，因此也有人称之为"石包玉"。河磨玉外包石皮，内分绿色、黄色和白色，其中黄白和白玉质最佳，其玉质纯净、坚韧、油脂感强，可与新疆和田玉相媲美。玉石在受沁的过程中，表面往往会形成一层氧化物，所以河磨玉一般会有红褐色以及黄褐色、土黄色和褐黑色等外皮。

考古发现研究证明，在辽宁省海城市小孤山仙人洞遗址，曾发掘出土距今1.2万年前的岫岩软玉砍斫器。此外分布在辽宁省西部及内蒙古东南部地区新石器时代中期的查海－兴隆洼文化、新石器时代晚期红山文化以及进入早期青铜时代的夏家店下层文化的先民们所使用玉器的材质，绝大多数为岫岩闪石玉。因此，鉴别古代玉器，认识其常用的材质是鉴定的基础。

第二，熟悉新石器时代及历史上各个时期玉器的造型特征和使用方法，是鉴定古代玉器的主要步骤。

在新石器时代，玉器的地域性是其主要特色。

红山文化玉器中的"C"形龙、猪龙、马蹄形箍、勾云形器、鸮、双龙首璜等特色鲜明，为其他史前时期考古学文化所不见。虽然其中的部分玉器的使用功能在学术界争论较大，但这些代表性玉器的原始宗教性与氏族首领的特权性是密不可分的。因此，鉴定红山文化玉器时，必须清楚在这一考古学文化中都有哪些类型玉器的存在，它们的大小尺寸的变化，造型中的细枝末节，并从考古学报告中分析研究每一类器形的使用方法、使用的多寡以及它们的材质区别等容易被别人忽略之处，形成自己的一套鉴别方法。

第三，时代背景下的时代风格是鉴定古代玉器的一把钥匙。

玉器是社会发展到一定阶段的产物，因此把握同一时期人们的精神文化的状况，才能理解为什么某类型的玉器产生在此阶段而非彼阶段，进而了解这一时期玉器的总体时代风格。

红山文化时期的人们正处于迈向中华文明的门槛阶段，玉"C"形龙、猪龙、"Y"形器、勾云形器等特殊造型，都是当时精神文化状况的直接反应，而绝非是人们头脑一时的发热冲动和杜撰。现今人们没有体验当时人们的精神世界，因而也就不可能真正创造出符合当时人们心理的玉器，所以除了刻意模仿和臆测别无他法，所制作的"红山文化玉器"就会不伦不类，最多是形似而已。因此，研究并了解古代玉器产生的时代背景，对于学习者鉴定古代玉器是十分重要的。

第四，玉器的纹饰以及残留的制作痕迹是最直观的鉴别依据。

古人制作玉器时，纹饰的制作绝非仅仅追求好看，而绝大多数有其特殊的内在含义，越是久远的就越是如此。而由于古代玉器制作年代久远，没有保留全套完整的加工器具给后人了解，文字记载玉器加工的程序和方法也仅仅是明代中晚期以后的事，距今也就几百年而已。所以残存在玉器表面的任何痕迹都是研究古代玉器制作的最佳线索，因此也就成为鉴定古玉的有力依据。

红山文化时期玉器的雕琢工艺十分讲究，特色鲜明，玉器表面很少装饰纹样，个别的如"C"形龙的额部的网状方格纹，猪龙眼、耳、嘴部雕琢的线纹，勾云形器上镂空与打洼技法表现的"眉"、"眼"、"牙"等，经认真观察研究发现，这些纹样应具有特殊的含义，制作这些纹样则有一套成熟的程序与工具；玉鸮、玉蝉蛹等打孔痕迹，玉箍的中空取料痕迹，均是研究红山文化玉器的制作工具与技法的最好实证。

还有在古玉真伪辨别方面，有实践经验和认知水平高的鉴赏家，他们的看法也值得借鉴。如所谓的"包浆"、"手头"、"老玉新工"等。

包浆：包浆一词在清代文献中已存在，应指玉器表面的皮壳特点，形成的原因很多，主要为沁色和盘色，沁色指玉器埋在地下，或传世过程中，由于受周围环境的影响（包括埋藏环境、保存条件等）在玉器表面形成的一层颜色变化，多见白色、铁锈色、暗黄色、黑色、绿色，白色多称水沁，铁锈色有人称铁锈沁，有人称血沁，暗黄色称土沁，沁色形成的原因很复杂，大体沿玉器染色与风化过程形成，又因玉器埋藏的时代不同、地区不同而不同，一般看，汉代以前玉器沁色较重，南方出土玉器称为湿土出土玉器，水沁较重。红山玉器被一些人称为北方燥土出土玉器，或无沁，或白色沁，或铁锈沁，或暗黄色沁，沁色一般都较少，少量玉器为较重的白色或褐色沁。

手头：一般指玉器拿在手中的重量感。与玻璃和塑料等仿玉材料相比，玉料的密度较大，即手头较重。许多仿玉大多在器形、纹饰、颜色、亮度等各方面都可以惟妙惟肖，但拿在手里一掂，却轻飘飘的。

手感：是指玉对温度变化惰性的性质，常见玉料绝大部分是晶质集合体，有较好的传热性，所以手摸玉器，会有冰凉感。但有些仿品系用玻璃或塑料制成，用手摸，很快冰凉感即消失。

光亮：玉器光亮有两种，一种叫"胶亮"，指玉件过完胶砣后，不用抛光罩亮直接上蜡。而"高亮"，指玉件过完胶砣后，先用抛光粉罩亮，再上蜡。

老玉新工：是指现代人利用古代出土玉器或遗留下来的老玉料、古玉残件等重新加工改制成的玉器。在造型、纹饰、工艺特点都符合古玉器时代特征时，还要进行玉器是否为仿制的判定，这主要在于对玉器新旧的理解。

另外，应该积极引进自然科学方法，来判断玉的材料、产地及琢玉工艺。自从引进扫描电子显微镜照相、中红外光谱测定、近红外光谱测定等物理学方法，玉材的显微结构和矿物组成问题得到了解决。对新疆和田、青海昆仑山、辽宁岫岩、河南南阳、台东花莲等著名产玉区矿物组成的测定，为出土古代玉器材料产地的确定提供了可靠地对比资料，再有模拟实验和微痕研究，则解决了长期以来有关线切割和砣切割、手刻及砣刻的争论。

总之，古代玉器的鉴定，包括理论与实践结合两个方面，经过较长时间的实际摸索，找出其历史发展的规律，进而总结出一套切合实际的方法，并在实践中不断总结，不被固有的信条束缚，才能有所突破，有所建树。

APPENDIX:

BASIC METHODS OF JADES IDENTIFYING

◎ Hong Dianxu

To identify ancient Chinese jades, it is significant not only to understand basic traits of jades like the existing region in each historical period and their morphology, but also to read archaeological reports about unearthed jades and consult formal jade catalogues published by famous museums or archaeological institutes. More important is to directly observe ancient jade objects preserved in museums in terms of their details such as material, shape, decoration and carving techniques and therefore establish a systematic and practical method for jade identification based on previous experience.

First of all, we need to be familiar with the characteristics of jade materials in all Neolithic archaeological cultures and the historical periods, especially the physical properties of common jade materials, such as the texture, color, hardness, transparency, and gloss, which can give us a better understanding of the choice of raw materials. For example, jades of Hongshan Culture were usually made of tremolite from the Xiuyan County regions in Liaoning Province, including the so-called "old jade" and "river jade".

There are two types of old jade according to the origin: primary ore and secondary ore. The primary ore refers to tremolite jade material extracted from primary ore on the hilltop of Xiyugou in Xiuyan County. The jade is called "old" because of the aged ore pits for jade excavation on the hilltop that suggests a long history of excavation and it is thus distinguished from the serpentine jade, the common-sense Xiuyan jade, and were mainly excavated from Wagou.

River jade is secondary ore old jade, which refers to tremolite jade from the sides of Xiyugou valley, Baisha River valley near Xiyugou, and the layer of earth and gravel on the river terrace. About billions of years ago, original jade rocks on the hilltop of Xiyugou turned into stones of diverse sizes during weathering. After being flushed into the river, the jade stones were gradually rubbed into smooth and rounded pebbles due to friction with other stones. A brown, sienna, sandy brown, or dark brown stone skin—an oxide layer in fact—was formed on the surface after weathering and earth infiltration. Therefore, the river jade was also called "jade in stone".

The jade cores of river pebbles are usually in colors of green, yellow, or white, with the ones in yellowish white and pure white being the best for their purity, toughness, and glossiness. They even rival the famous Hotan jade from Xinjiang. Xiuyan nephrite choppers that date to 12,000 years ago were unearthed at the Xianrendong site in Haicheng, Liaoning Province.

Other archaeological discoveries show that the raw materials of jade objects of many archaeological cultures were mostly Xiuyan tremolite jade, including findings from the middle Neolithic Chahai-Xinglongwa Culture in western Liaoning and southeastern Inner Mongolia, the upper Neolithic Hongshan Culture, and early Bronze lower Xiajiadian Culture. Therefore, the understanding of jade materials is the foundation of ancient jade identification.

Secondly, the characteristics in appearance and function of jade from Neolithic Age and each historical period are the main clues for ancient jade identification. Regionality is the main feature of Neolithic jades. The typical Hongshan Culture jades, like C-shaped dragon, pig-dragon, hoof-shaped jade, jade in the shape of hook and cloud, jade owl, and huang semicircle with two dragon heads, all have distinctive characteristics that are usually absent in other prehistoric archaeological cultures. Although there is still controversy in the academic circle about some of their functions, it is undoubted that these representative jade objects are closely related to primitive religious beliefs and tribe leaders' prerogative. Therefore, to identify a Hongshan Culture jade, it is crucial to understand the Hongshan Culture jade types and the differences in size and design. It is also important to analyze the sometimes ignored information from archaeological reports, such as the application of each jade type, frequency of its use, and materials.

Thirdly, jade style based on the historical context is a key to the identification. Jades were manufactured as the society progressed into a certain stage and only when we comprehend the ideology of that time can we understand why some type of jade was produced then and furthermore grasp the overall style of jades of that period. The Hongshan Culture was in the transitional stage to the dawn of Chinese civilization. Unique shapes of jade, such as C-shaped dragon, pig-dragon, Y-shaped objects, and the objects in the shape of hook and cloud, are all direct reflection of the ideology of that time rather than impulsive creation. Having no experience of the ancestors' internal expression, modern people can not manufacture jades that are coordinated with the ancient psychology. They could do nothing but imitate and purely conjecture and the produced; "Hongshan Culture jades" are anomalous and no more than similar in shape. Therefore, the study of time background is significant for the identification of ancient jades.

Fourthly, the decorative patterns and remained manufacturing traces are the direct evidence for the identification. The patterns on ancient jades are not only for decoration, but also have special implication—the more aged the jade is, the more so. Since the manufacture of ancient jades was too long ago to leave any complete set of processing tools for nowadays research and written records about jades processing procedure and technique only document those after the mid-Ming Dynasty, which was just hundreds of years ago, traces remaining on the jade surface become the best evidence to study ancient jade manufacturing and for their identification.

There are seldom decorative patterns on Hongshan Culture jades. Close observations show that some patterns, namely the grid lines in the forehead of the C-shaped dragon, the engraved lines in the eyes, ears, and mouth of the pig-dragon, and the hollowed and grooved eyebrow, eye, and teeth in the hook-and-cloud-shaped pendant, all have special implications and they must have been made with a mature procedure and kit. The traces of drilling on the jade owl and the jade silkworm chrysalis and those of hollowing on the jade hoop are all perfect information to study the Hongshan Culture jades manufacturing tools and techniques.

Besides, viewpoints of the experienced and knowledgeable connoisseurs are important references for the ancient jade identification, such as the so-called "patina", "weight by hand", and "old jade with new processing". Patina first appeared in the early Qing Dynasty documents. It indicates the unique rind of jades and can be divided into environmental-infiltrated and touching-infiltrated color according to the formation mechanism. Environmental-infiltrated color refers to the color change on the jade surface when it is influenced by the environment (including burial and preservation conditions) when it is buried underground or being handed down over a long time span. Environmental-infiltrated colors are usually white, rusty, sienna, black, or green. The white is called water-infiltrated; the rusty is called rust-infiltrated or blood-infiltrated, while the sienna is called earth-infiltrated. The formation of environmental-infiltrated color is complex, mostly caused by the pigmentation and weathering and differs as the burial time and region of jades changes. Generally speaking, jades before the Han Dynasty had heavier environmental-infiltrated color. Jades unearthed from south China, which are called wet-soil-unearthed jades, have a heavy water-infiltrated color. Hongshan jades, called by some people the northern dry-soil-unearthed jades, commonly have slight environmental-infiltrated colors of white, rusty, or sienna. Some Hongshan jades have no such infiltrated color and only a few of them have comparatively heavy white or brown environmental-infiltrated color.

Weight by hand literally refers to the weight of jades measured by hand. Compared with counterfeit jade materials like glass and plastic, jade has a higher density and feels heavier at hand. Most of the counterfeit jade can be paralleled with authentic ones in shape, pattern, color, and brightness, but never in density. When held in hand, counterfeits feel far less heavy.

Hand feel indicates the feel of jade, which reflects the jade inertia to the change of temperature. Normal jade materials are crystalline aggregate and have good diathermancy and they usually feel cool when touched by hand. On the contrary, the coolness of some counterfeit jades made of crystal, glass, or plastic will instantly disappear.

Gloss, or polishing in the modern concept: there are two kinds of jade gloss, one is "resin polishing" and the other is "highlighted polishing". "Resin polishing" refers to a polishing process in which jades are directly waxed after being polished by the resin wheel and this method is mostly applied in manufacturing of ancient jade imitation. While there is an extra step in "highlighted polishing"—the application of a polishing powder coat before waxing.

Old jade with new processing refers to jades that modern people make from excavated ancient jades, handed-down ones, or ancient jade shards by reprocessing. Additionally, when a jade object is in accordance with ancient jades in terms of shape, decorative pattern, and technique, it is still necessary to clarify if it is imitated based on the thorough understanding of ancient jades characteristics.

What's more, methods in natural science should be actively applied to identify jade's material, origin and jade carving techniques. Since the application of methods in physics, such as scanning electron photomicrograph, mid-infrared spectrometry and near-infrared spectrometry, the problem of microstructure and mineral composition of jade materials have been solved. Through the measurement of mineral composition of jade in famous mines, such as Hetian in Xinjiang Autonomous Region, Kunlun Mountains in Qinghai Province, Xiuyan in Liaoning Province, Nanyang in Henan Province and Hualian in eastern Taiwan, reliable sources for comparison have been offered in the determination of origin of ancient jade materials unearthed. Besides, simulation experiments and study on micro mark have put an end to the arguments about line cutting, thallium cutting, hand carving and thallium carving.

In conclusion, the identification of ancient jade should be the combination of theory and practice. We need to grasp the historical regularity of jade characteristics, accumulate experience through practices, and meanwhile stay innovative. We need also sum up a methodology of our own.

后 记

◎ 洪殿旭

　　《红山文化玉器鉴赏》一书的策划和编写得到了国家文物局、北京市政府、辽宁省政府、内蒙古自治区政府和河北省政府有关部门领导、同仁的关怀以及社会有关方面的支持。

　　全国政协副主席白立忱始终热心关怀本书的出版工作。中国艺术研究院原副院长冯其庸先生为本书题写了书名。辽宁省政府原副省长林声、内蒙古自治区政协主席王占和中国书法研究院名誉院长欧阳中石热情为本书题词。

　　本书的成书得益于国家文物局局长单霁翔，副局长顾玉才、宋新潮、张柏，辽宁省文化厅厅长郭兴文，内蒙古自治区文化厅厅长王志城，辽宁省文物局原局长张春雨、局长丁辉、副局长李向东，内蒙古自治区文物局原局长刘兆和、局长安泳锝，天津市文物局局长张志，北京市文物局副局长于平，河北省文物局副局长谢飞、李恩佳，陕西省文物局副局长刘云辉，河南省文物局副局长孙英民，北京故宫博物院原院长于坚、常务副院长李季、副院长王亚民，中国国家博物馆副馆长董琦，北京市文物局副局长兼首都博物馆馆长郝东晨，中国社会科学院考古研究所所长王巍、副所长陈星灿，中国文物交流中心主任吴东风，天津博物馆原馆长云希正、馆长白文源，内蒙古博物院院长塔拉、副院长付宁，内蒙古自治区文化厅文物处处长王大方，赤峰市文化局局长陶建英，辽宁省文物考古所原所长田立坤、所长吴炎亮，辽宁省博物馆馆长马宝杰，河北省文物考古研究所所长韩立森，赤峰市博物馆馆长刘冰，朝阳市博物馆馆长尚晓波，阜新市博物馆馆长胡健，张家口市博物馆馆长姚玉柱，内蒙古敖汉旗博物馆馆长田彦国，内蒙古巴林右旗博物馆馆长石阳，中国收藏家协会名誉会长闫振堂、会长罗伯健，中国文物学会会长彭卿云，中国文物保护基金会理事长马自树，中国考古学会会长张忠培，国家文物鉴定委员会主任委员傅熹年、副主任委员耿宝昌，中国文物学会玉器委员会会长杨伯达、副会长卢兆荫，北京大学考古文博学院院长赵辉、原常务副院长赵朝洪、著名考古学家及博士生导师严文明、台北故宫博物院院长冯明珠、器物处处长邓淑苹和香港中文大学中国考古艺术研究中心原主任杨建芳等领导、专家、学者及同仁的大力支持和协助，在此表示感谢！

此外，向所有支持本书出版的国内外博物馆、考古所、研究机构、发行专家、学者和同仁致以诚挚的谢意。并感谢美国华盛顿沙可乐博物馆Keith Wilson副馆长、Christine Lee女士、程薇娜女士，芝加哥博物馆Elinor Pearlstein副馆长，旧金山亚洲艺术博物馆Aino Tolme先生，英国大英博物馆Carol Michaelson副主任，法国国立吉美博物馆Tsao Huei –Uhung研究员以及台北、香港鉴赏家何鸿卿、霍丽娜、钟华培和徐政夫等提供的协助。

文物出版社名誉社长苏士澍、社长张自成、总编辑葛承雍、责任编辑张征雁为本书如期出版付出了辛勤的劳动，在此一并致谢。

书中所述红山文化是在中国辽宁省西部、内蒙古东南部和河北省西北部发现的一种考古学文化，距今6500~5000年。其中20世纪80年代中期以来发掘的朝阳市牛河梁红山文化女神庙、祭坛、积石冢遗址，被学者认为是中华五千年文明史起源的象征。红山文化内涵丰富，玉器是其中的重要组成部分。

本书是在郭大顺和洪殿旭的主持下编撰而成的，因此本书是集体研究成果的结晶和体现。编者注意吸纳和整合学术界已有的研究成果，收录的213件红山文化玉器，多发掘于辽宁西部、内蒙古东部和河北北部地区，是由国内外专业博物馆和考古所提供的，具有毋庸置疑的可靠性和真实性，并具有权威性。希望本书的出版对红山文化玉器的研究起到推动作用。

ACKNOWLEDGEMENTS

◎ Hong Dianxu

This book is written with the generous supports from the State Administration of Cultural Heritage, Beijing Municipal Government, Liaoning Provincial Government, Inner Mongolia Autonomous Region Government, Hebei Provincial Government, colleagues, friends, and the general public.

Vice-chairman of Chinese People's Political Consultative Conference, Bai Lichen expresses his warm-hearted concern about the publication of the book.The Chinese characters of the book title are handwritten by Mr. Feng Qiyong, former Vice President of China Art Academy. The forewords are written by Mr. Lin Sheng, former Vice Governor of Liaoning Province, Mr. Wang Zhan, Chairman of Inner Mongolia Autonomous Region Political Consultative Conference, and Mr. Ouyang Zhongshi, Honorary Director of Institute of Chinese Calligraphy. The authors would like to give our thanks to the following people:

Shan Jixiang, Director General of State Administration of Cultural Heritage;

Gu Yucai, Deputy Director General of State Administration of Cultural Heritage;

Song Xinchao, Deputy Director General of State Administration of Cultural Heritage;

Zhang Bai, Deputy Director General of State Administration of Cultural Heritage;

Guo Xingwen, Director of Liaoning Provincial Department of Culture;

Wang Zhicheng, Director of Inner Mongolia Autonomous Region Department of Culture;

Zhang Chunyu, former Director of Liaoning Provincial Bureau of Cultural Relics;

Ding Hui, Director of Liaoning Provincial Bureau of Cultural Relics;

Li Xiangdong, Deputy Director of Liaoning Provincial Bureau of Cultural Relics;

Liu Zhaohe, former Director of Inner Mongolia Autonomous Region Bureau of Cultural Relics;

An Yongde, Director of Inner Mongolia Autonomous Region Bureau of Cultural Relics;

Zhang Zhi, Director of Tianjin Municipal Bureau of Cultural Relics;

Yu Ping, Deputy Director of Beijing Municipal Bureau of Cultural Relics;

Xie Fei, Deputy Director of Hebei Provincial Bureau of Cultural Relics;

Li Enjia, Deputy Director of Hebei Provincial Bureau of Cultural Relics;

Liu Yunhui, Deputy Director of Shaanxi Provincial Bureau of Cultural Relics;

Sun Yingmin, Deputy Director of Henan Provincial Bureau of Cultural Relics;

Yu Jian, former Director of the Palace Museum, Beijing;

Li Ji, Executive Deputy Director of the Palace Museum, Beijing;

Wang Yamin, Deputy Director of the Palace Museum, Beijing;

Dong Qi, Deputy Director of the National Museum of China;

Hao Dongchen, Deputy Director of Beijing Municipal Administration of Cultural Heritage and Director of the Capital Museum;

Wang Wei, Director of Institute of Archaeology, Chinese Academy of Social Sciences;

Chen Xingcan, Deputy Director of Institute of Archaeology, Chinese Academy of Social Sciences;

Wu Dongfeng, Director of China Cultural Heritage Exchange Center;

Yun Xizheng, former Director of Tianjin Museum;

Bai Wenyuan, Director of Tianjin Museum;

Tara, Director of Museum of Inner Mongolia Autonomous Region;

Fu Ning, Deputy Director of Museum of Inner Mongolia Autonomous Region;

Wang Dafang, Director of Cultural Relics, Inner Mongolia Autonomous Region Department of Culture;

Tao Jianying, Director of Chifeng Department of Culture;

Tian Likun, former Director of Liaoning Provincial Institute of Cultural Relics and Archaeology;

Wu Yanling, Director of Liaoning Provincial Institute of Cultural Relics and Archaeology;

Ma Baojie, Director of Museum of Liaoning Province;

Han Lisen, Director of Hebei Provincial Institute of Cultural Relics and Archaeology;

Liu Bing, Director of Chifeng Museum, Inner Mongolia;

Shang Xiaobo, Director of Chaoyang Museum, Liaoning;

Hu Jian, Director of Fuxin Museum, Liaoning;

Yao Yuzhu, Director of Zhangjiakou Museum, Hebei;

Tian Yanguo, Director of Aohan Banner Museum, Inner Mongolia;

Shi Yang, Director of Bairin Right Banner Museum, Inner Mongolia;

Yan Zhentang, Honorary President of China Association of Collectors;

Luo Bojian, President of China Association of Collectors;

Peng Qingyun, President of Chinese Society of Cultural Relics;

Ma Zishu, President of China Cultural Relics Protection Foundation;

Zhang Zhongpei, former President of Chinese Society of Archaeology;

Fu Xinian, Director of State Committee of Cultural Relics Authentication;

Geng Baochang, Deputy Director of State Committee of Cultural Relics Authentication;

Yang Boda, Chairperson of Jade, Chinese Society of Cultural Relics;

Lu Zhaoyin, Deputy Chairperson of Jade, Chinese Society of Cultural Relics;

Zhao Hui, Director of School of Archaeology and Museology, Peking University

Zhao Chaohong, former Executive Deputy Director of School of Archaeology and Museology, Peking University;

Yan Wenming, famous archaeologist and PH.D.supervisor;

Feng Mingzhu, Director of the Palace Museum, TaiPei;

Teng Shu-p'ing, Director of Antiquities, Palace Museum, Taipei;

Yeung Kin-fong, former Director of Centre for Chinese Archaeology and Art, Chinese University of Hong Kong; and many other scholars, friends, and colleagues who have aided in the project.

The authors are also grateful to museums, institutes, scholars, and friends who offered their help in publishing this book. Special thanks go to Deputy Director, Mr. Keith Wilson, Ms. Christine Lee, and Ms. Weina Tray of Arthur M. Sackler Gallery in Washington, Deputy Director, Ms. Elinor Pearlstein of Art Institute of Chicago, Mr. Aino Tolme of Asian Art Museum of San Francisco in the U.S.A., Ms. Carol Michaelson of the British Museum in Britain, Ms. Tsao Huei-chung of Musée Guimet in France, Mr.Ho Hung-hing, Ms.Fog Lai-nar, Mr.Zhong Huapei and Mr.Xu Zhengfu, Connoisseurs and Collectors in Hong Kong and Taipei. The authors express their sincere thanks to Honorary Director Su Shishu, Director Zhang Zicheng, Editor-in-Chief Ge Chengyong, and Editor/Reviser Zhang Zhengyan of Cultural Relics Press for their hard efforts in making sure that this book is published in time.

The Hongshan Culture that this book focuses on is a type of archaeological culture that dates to 6,000-5,000 years ago. Its remains are discovered in China's western Liaoning Province, southeastern Inner Mongolia Autonomous Region, and northwestern Hebei Province. Among those cultural remains, the Goddess Temple, altar, and stone tomb complex found at Niuheliang in Chaoyang, Liaoning Province in the middle 1980s are believed by scholars to be the symbol of the origins of 5,000-year Chinese civilization. Hongshan Culture is known for rich contents and jades are one of its most important parts. This book is written under the supervision of Guo Dashun and Hong Dianxu and is a product of collaborative research. By absorbing existing research findings, the authors introduce altogether 213 Hongshan Culture jades, mostly unearthed in western Liaoning, eastern Inner Mongolia and northern Hebei. These jades come from museums and institutes from China and abroad and offer reliable sources. It is hoped that this book could push forward the studies on Hongshan Culture jades.

Handwriting of Book Title: Feng Qiyong (former Vice President of China Art Academy and honorary Director of Research Institute of Chinese Culture of Renmin University of China)

Photographers: Kong Qun, Sun Li, Dong Qing, Ji Lianqi, Lin Li, Hu Chui, Liu Zhigang, Pang Lei

Editors: Zhang Wenfang, Cui Yanqin, Chen Wei

English Translators: Li Jinghui, Zhang Hai, Xia Meifang, Wang Hongmin, Carol Michaelson, Guo Ming, Guo Jianning, Bjmal Shal, Zhao Jing

Managing Editor: Xu Yang

Typographical Designer: Xu Yang

Managing Printer: Su Lin

A STUDY OF HONGSHAN CULTURE JADES (Enlarged Edition)

Edited by: Guo Dashun, Hong Dianxu

Published and Distributed by: CULTURAL RELICS PRESS

2 beixiaojie, dongzhimennei, Beijing 100007

http://www.wenwu.com

E-mail: web@wenwu.com

Printed by: CULTURAL RELICS PRESS PRINTING CO., LTD.

Distributed by: XINHUA BOOKSTORE

Internationally Distributed by: CHINA INTERNATIONAL BOOK TRADING CORPORATION

Dimension: 889mm×1194mm 1/16

Printed Sheets: 15.75

Edition: first edition January 2014

Printing: second printing May 2020

Book Number: ISBN 978-7-5010-3912-8

Price: 480.00RMB

All Rights Reserved.

书名题签：冯其庸（中国艺术研究院原副院长、现任中国人民大学国学院名誉院长、国学大师）

摄　　影：孔　群　孙　力　董　清　季连琪

　　　　　　林　利　胡　锤　刘志岗　庞　雷

编　　务：张文芳　崔岩勤　陈　为

英文翻译：李竞辉　张　海　夏美芳　王洪敏

　　　　　　Carol Mtchaelson　郭　明　郭建宁

　　　　　　Bimal Shal　赵　静

责任编辑：徐　旸

版式设计：徐　旸

责任印制：苏　林

图书在版编目（CIP）数据

红山文化玉器鉴赏 / 郭大顺，洪殿旭编著. -- 增订

本. -- 北京：文物出版社，2014.1（2020.5 重印）

ISBN 978-7-5010-3912-8

Ⅰ. ①红… Ⅱ. ①郭… ②洪… Ⅲ. ①红山文化－古

玉器－鉴赏－中国 Ⅳ. ①K876.84

中国版本图书馆CIP数据核字(2013)第282037号

红山文化玉器鉴赏（增订本）

郭大顺　洪殿旭　编著

文物出版社出版发行

　　（北京市东直门内北小街2号楼　邮编：100007）

　　http://www.wenwu.com

　　E-mail:web@wenwu.com

制版印刷　文物出版社印刷厂有限公司

经　　销　新华书店

国外发行　中国图书进出口（集团）公司

开　　本　889×1194毫米　1/16

印　　张　15.75

版　　次　2014年1月第1版

印　　次　2020年5月第1版2次印刷

书　　号　ISBN 978-7-5010-3912-8

定　　价　480.00元

本书版权独家所有，非经授权，不得复制翻印